ALL YOU NEED TO KNOW ABOUT

WINEMAKING

Marshall Cavendish

Contents

Editor: Alison Louw
Designer: Judith Robertson
Illustrator: Sue Richards
Stylist: Jane Fletcher
Cover photograph: Melvin Grey

Published by Marshall Cavendish Limited
58 Old Compton Street
London W1V 5PA

© Marshall Cavendish Limited 1985

Printed and bound in Italy by
New Interlitho SpA.

ISBN 0 86307 217 8

Wine 1
About home winemaking

Wine has been made in the home for many centuries and, as commercial wines become more and more expensive, interest in this ancient domestic art is reviving. Excellent wines can be made in the home from virtually any non-toxic fruit, vegetable, grain and flower, in fresh, canned or dried form — even tea or the sap from a tree can be used for winemaking!

Not only is home winemaking very cheap and an excellent way of using up surplus produce, but many people are discovering delicious and exotic flavours which they prefer to the grape. Also, by making your own wine you can evolve one exactly suited to your palate.

For those who still prefer the taste of grape wine, grape juice concentrates have become freely available from the many home winemakers' stores; with these, commercial-type wines can be emulated. The stores also stock all types of grain, dried and canned fruits and vegetables that are suitable for winemaking, together with all the necessary equipment and additives. The same equipment is used over and over again, so that once the initial outlay has been made only the ingredients are required.

Winemaking and the law

Home winemaking is allowed in most countries but is usually for home consumption only. In some countries you need a permit which is usually free and easy to obtain and sometimes it is forbidden to take the wine off the premises. The laws differ in minor details from country to country and in the United States of America from state to state. So, if in any doubt, any reputable home-brewer's store will help.

NELSON HARGREAVES

Wine 2 Contents & theory

Content

Wine comes either dry, medium or sweet, and is a mixture of water, alcohol and flavouring agents — the bulk being water. (In winemaking 'dry' means 'not sweet'.)

The water comes from a tap and the alcohol is formed automatically during the fermentation process. But it is the flavour and aroma that gives wine its outstanding characteristics and which requires the most attention.

Wine can be made from almost anything that can be fermented but it is essential that certain ingredients be present for fermentation or flavour. All the essential ingredients are normally present in wine grapes but with other bases it may be necessary to add certain ingredients such as acid, tannin, yeast, sugar.

Yeast. The bloom on growing grapes is a yeast which is essential to the fermentation of wine. This has to be added to other fruits.

Sugar, which is needed for the action of yeast, is nearly always added. In varieties of grape which ripen late in the season the sugar content is usually sufficient.

So, to make wine, we extract the juices, known as the 'must', from the fermentable material, compensate for any deficiencies in flavour and essential ingredients, add yeast and sugar, and keep the fermentation vessel to the required temperature to encourage yeast action. Care must be taken to keep out any wild yeasts present in the atmosphere, acetobacters (vinegar-forming bacteria) and the vinegar fly. After a short while the must will start to froth and bubble—fermentation has started.

Medieval painting showing vineyard activities in autumn, Castello del Buonconsiglio Trento, Italy.

Yeast and fermentation

When the must ferments the yeast enzymes feed on sugar and convert it to ethyl alcohol and carbon dioxide gas. The yeast continues feeding on the sugar until **a** all the sugar is used up or **b** the alcohol content becomes so high that the yeast is killed and fermentation ceases — this happens when the alcohol content reaches between 10% and 17% by volume.

A deposit known as 'lees' will have formed on the bottom of the fermentation vessel.

If any sugar is left unconverted the wine will be sweet. One way of controlling the sugar is to add only sufficient sugar to produce the required alcohol content and to completely ferment this sugar, leaving a dry wine. Then, if a sweet wine is required, a sweetening agent can be added when fermentation has ceased.

Alcohol content

The alcohol content of wines is normally expressed as '% alcohol by volume'. Most table wines have between 10% and 12% alcohol, equivalent to the 10° and 12° seen on Continental wines. Aperitifs, ports, sherries and dessert wines are usually stronger — between 15% and 30% alcohol. Liqueurs are stronger still — ranging from 30% to 75%.

However, to add complications, there are other ways of measuring alcohol content as, for example, the British proof system, used in Canada, Australia, New Zealand, Ireland and the Republic of South Africa. To make matters even more complicated there are also the US proof and metric systems, the latter named Gay Lussac (G.L.) after its French originator. The following table compares these systems.

	British system	US system	Metric system (G.L.)	% alcohol
Absolute alcohol	175°	200°	100°	100
Normal spirit strength	70°	80°	40°	40
Table wine	17.5°	20°	10°	10°

Wine 3 Types & usage

Colour

Wines can be red, white or pink (rosé). Usually the colour of the wine will depend on the type of fruit used. However, with grapes it is the skins which give colour to the wine. Red grape wine can only be made from black grapes, the colour deriving from the skins; if the skins are removed as soon as the grapes are pressed a white wine results. Green grapes will produce only white wine. A rosé wine can be obtained from black grapes by leaving the skins in the pressed juice for a short while or by mixing red and white wines.

Types of wine

Wines, both sweet and dry, may be classified as Aperitifs, Table wines, Dessert wines and Liqueurs.

Aperitifs. As their name suggests, aperitifs are intended to stimulate the appetite and to get the digestive juices flowing. They are often, but not always, dry and astringent, with delicate flavours. Sherry is usually drunk as an aperitif.

Table wines form by far the largest category, and quantity, of wine. As the name suggests, these are the wines traditionally drunk at meal times. They may range from darkest red to almost colourless, from sweet to dry, but are usually classified according to colour as red, white and rosé.

All three classifications are produced in different grades of sweetness or dryness.

It is usual to drink a dry or medium white wine with white-fleshed meat such as chicken, fish, veal and pork, while a full-bodied red wine is widely preferred with red meats; rosé wines can be drunk with almost anything.

Dessert wines. These are rich, rather sweet, strongly flavoured wines such as Madeira, Muscatel or Port and are normally taken either with a sweet or pudding course or separately after a meal.

Mead can be made dry or sweet. It has honey as a base and is not to everyone's taste, but make some and try it. Mead can be drunk at any time, before, during or after meals.

Champagne and sparkling wines — the traditional drinks for weddings and celebrations — are bubbling and effervescent. Many home winemakers make very successful sparkling wines. But, before you try, a word of warning: the process of fermentation in the bottle which produces the bubbles can lead to great pressure in the bottles and result in nasty and dangerous explosions.

Fortification

This is the adding of alcohol to a wine either to arrest the fermentation and leave some unfermented sugar, or to give better keeping qualities to the wine, or simply to give the wine a higher alcohol content.

Table wines usually contain from 10% to 12% alcohol. Most aperitifs, dessert wines, Ports, Sherries and liqueurs have a higher alcohol content than this. To increase the alcohol content a wine has to be fortified by the addition of spirits. The home winemaker can use brandy or whisky or a neutral tasting spirit such as Vodka and Polish white spirit for making Port-style wines or liqueurs. The straight-forward fortification of some popular wines is included in the recipes.

Various ingredients and additives for making wine and mead. Note that pale honey is used. These scales are good for measuring very small quantities, such as the small amounts of tannin and citric acid required.

Wine 4 Basic ingredients

Winemakers' kits

If entirely new to winemaking you are strongly recommended to try your hand at one of the several 'winemakers' kits' now available. These kits contain everything needed, except sugar and water, to make 1 gallon (4.5 litres) or 5 gallons (23 litres), of wine. With some kits the container is designed to act both as a fermentation vessel and a storage container, complete with tap. The outlay is not large and the process is so designed that instructions are few and simple.

Wine concentrates

Concentrated grape juices. These include unspecified white and red grape juices and many named varieties including Hock, Burgundy, Bordeaux, Chablis,. Chianti, Claret, Sauternes, Port, Sherry and Vermouth. The cans normally contain 2lb 3oz (1 kg) and are sufficient to make 1 gallon (4.5 litres) of wine; larger cans containing up to 1 gallon (4.5 litres) of concentrate are also available.
The concentrates also vary in quality and price. Some mention the country of origin — Spanish, Italian, French; the term 'other Mediterranean' usually means either Algerian, Cypriot or Moroccan, all large producers of excellent wines.

Other concentrates available include apricot, bilberry, cherry, elderberry, peach and various combinations such as grape and bilberry. These concentrates are also sold in 2lb 3oz (1 kg) cans or larger.

Fruits and other wine bases

Canned fruits are available as pieces, pulps and purées, often in 4lb (1.8 kg) cans, or larger. Varieties include apple, apricot, bilberry, blackberry, gooseberry, pineapple, prune and rhubarb. These cans are good value for those who make wines in quantities larger than 1 gallon (4.5 litres).

Dried fruits. Most winemakers' stores carry a good stock of dried apricots, bananas, bilberries, elderberries and flowers, dates, figs, peaches, rose hips, raisins and sultanas (white raisins). Buy the seedless or stoned varieties of raisins and sultanas if possible.

Fresh fruits. The fresh fruits often used in winemaking include apples, bilberries, blueberries, blackcurrants, cherries (morello), damsons, elderberries, gooseberries, grapes, greengages, lemons, loganberries, oranges, peaches, pears, pineapples, plums, pomegranate, quinces, raspberries, redcurrants, strawberries and whitecurrants — the range is endless. Use only fresh fruit as stored (refrigerated) fruit soon loses its flavour. The fruit should be well ripened and, if at all possible, picked on a warm, sunny day.

Fresh flowers. Fresh flowers have been used in winemaking for many years. These include broom, carnation, cowslip, dandelion, elderflower, gorse, hawthorn, honeysuckle, marigold, pansy, primrose, rose petals and wallflower. Gather them on a dry day, when they are free from morning or evening dew.

Grains, leaves, herbs and sap. Barley, corn (maize), wheat and rice are some of the grains used; for the other categories, balm, blackberry shoot, burdock, coltsfoot, fennel, lemon thyme, mint, nettle, oakleaf, parsley, sage, vine shoot, walnut leaf, birch and sycamore sap may be encountered.

Beverages, nuts, spices, preserves. The following may be used: almond, clove, coffee, ginger, honey, malt, tea, vanilla.

Fresh vegetables. Both the more common and more exotic vegetables may be found on the winemakers' shelves: Jerusalem artichoke, aubergine (eggplant), beetroot (beet), broad bean, cabbage, carrot, celery, kohl rabi, mangold, marrow, parsnip, peapod, potato, pumpkin, rhubarb, sugar beet, tomato, turnip. The above list is by no means complete — wine has been made from grass cuttings before now.

Sap and how to extract it

A sweet sap, suitable for winemaking, can be extracted from birch, sycamore and walnut trees in the last weeks of winter while the sap

is rising and just before buds are visible. The extraction procedure is as follows:

1 Operate only on mature trees at least 9 inches (230 mm) in diameter; if the tree is not yours, obtain permission first!

2 About 18 inches to 2 feet ($\frac{1}{2}$ to $\frac{2}{3}$ m) above the ground, drill a $\frac{1}{4}$-inch (6 mm) hole, slanting upwards, about one inch (25 mm) deep, no more, so that only the sapwood is penetrated.

3 Insert a plastic tube, as tight a fit as possible, about $\frac{3}{4}$ inch (20 mm) into the hole. The tube should be long enough to reach into a covered pail firmly supported on, or partly sunk into, the ground. The output of sap is higher than might be expected and the pail may fill in two days. However, 1 to $1\frac{1}{2}$ gallons ($4\frac{1}{2}$ to 7 litres) is enough for a tree to bear in a single year.

4 Strain the sap if necessary; if the juice is not going to be used immediately add two crushed Campden tablets per gallon (4.5 litres) and keep it in a closed container.

5 After the extraction, hammer in a tightly fitting length of dowelling to plug the hole.

Poisonous plants and insecticides

As some fruits and flowers are poisonous, the general rule is not to make wine of any fruit that is not normally eaten fresh, canned or dried. Apart from well known poisonous plants such as deadly nightshade and many fungi, the safe rule is to avoid using any plant unless you have a tried recipe for it.

Beware of picking flowers, leaves or plants that could have been sprayed with weedkiller as some modern weedkillers are highly poisonous. In any case fresh ingredients should always be thoroughly washed before use.

Other ingredients

The other essential ingredients are listed below; more detailed explanations of their usage will be found in the 'Methods' Chapter and, where necessary, in individual recipes.

Yeast. Yeast is essential to any winemaking. Although Baker's yeast can be used it is really

Grapes growing in River Douro Valley, Portugal.

intended for baking purposes; for the best results use a dried or liquid wine yeast specially made for the purpose. Yeasts which are not acceptable are the Brewer's types and wild yeasts whose spores are usually present in the air we breathe.

There are many varieties of cultured wine yeasts — Sherry, Madeira, Champagne, Port, Burgundy, Chablis and Beaujolais — in addition to an 'all-purpose' culture. It is noteworthy that one leading supplier has removed all the named varieties from his catalogue and is supplying the 'all-purpose' wine yeast only, his opinion being that other factors, particularly the grape juice or other main ingredient, affect the flavour of the finished wine to a far greater degree than the yeast, under home producing conditions. However, it is worth trying some of these yeasts to see if you agree. And a cereal yeast is always advisable with cereal wines to deal with the starch content.

Yeast nutrients and energizers. Some grape musts and certain others supply their own acids, nitrogen, salts and vitamins that the yeast needs to feed on. Most other musts are lacking in some of these elements and they have to be added artificially. It is possible to buy yeast nutrient and energizer in a combined form.

Sugar. Nearly all recipes call for the addition of sugar. Ordinary white granulated sugar is normally used. When wines need sweetening after fermentation has finished, lactose, which will not ferment, can be added, but many winemakers use the ordinary granulated sugar for this purpose.

A few recipes call for brown, or demerara, sugar where some stronger flavour is required, but its use is not essential.

Acids. Citric, tartaric or malic acids are required if a wine is to have a well balanced flavour. Some fruits such as grapes and apples usually have enough while other fruits such as bilberries and cherries need some acid added. Citric acid is usually used to make up any deficiency — one ounce of citric acid is equal to the juice of eight lemons and is very

much cheaper. Tartaric acid is sometimes used; it imparts a somewhat harsher flavour than citric acid but some people prefer it in wines.

Tannin is also a necessary ingredient of wine— without it, wines, which are normally slightly astringent, taste insipid. Too much tannin on the other hand, makes a wine too astringent. It is present in some fruits and leaves and in all grape juices. Grape tannin is available in both powder and liquid form.

Pectin destroying enzymes. Some fruits contain pectin, which, although desirable in jam making, causes cloudiness in wine. Depectinizers are then added to the must before fermentation. These are marked under various brand names such as Pectolase, Pectinol and Pectozyme.

Depectinizers inhibit the action of yeast — so wait at least 24 hours before adding the yeast.

Campden tablets. These are multipurpose tablets used for the sterilization of equipment, inhibiting mould growths in must and as a preservative of finished wines. Campden tablets do add a taste to wine but this wears off with ageing.

The active ingredient is sodium metabisulphite, which is also obtainable in powder form and may be marketed under another brand name.

Campden tablets inhibit the action of yeast — so wait at least 24 hours before adding the yeast.

Flavours, spices, herbs

Spices and herbs have long been used to impart various flavours to vermouth and other aperitif wines as well as mulled wines. Ginger is also used in some wines.

Flavouring essences. Special essences, formulated for winemakers, are available for those making liqueurs.

Various stages of wine, from grapes and additives to the finished product.

Wine 5
Basic equipment

The basic equipment needed for home wine-making is extremely simple and costs very little. Some of the articles needed will already be found in the home.

Here is a list of the equipment needed:

1 Boiling container — at least 2 gallon (9 litre) capacity.

2 Plastic pail — at least 2 gallon (9 litre) capacity.

3 Fermentation and storage jars—one gallon (4.5 litre) capacity.

4 Airlock for each fermentation jar.

5 Bored rubber bungs for airlocks.

6 Plain bungs to fit fermentation jars for storage.

7 A siphon tube — at least 4 feet (1.2 m) long.

8 Wine bottles.

9 Corks — for the wine bottles.

10 Corking tool — not essential but a great help.

11 Nylon sieve — at least 6 inches (152 mm) diameter.

12 Funnel — at least 6 inches (152 mm) diameter.

13 Hydrometer—not essential but you must have one if you want consistent results.

Acceptable materials

Acceptable materials for boiling and soaking vessels are: aluminium, stainless steel, un-chipped enamel, glazed pottery and colourless or white plastic (polythene).

Acceptable materials for fermentation and storage containers are: glass, colourless or white plastic (polythene) and, with reservations, wooden casks.

Note: do not use iron, steel, copper and brass as these will spoil your wine. Do not use scrat-

Straining strawberry must. The strainer bag hangs on a metal frame.

ched glazes or glazes with lead in them. Use white or colourless plastic as some colours have proved to be toxic, particularly yellow.

About the equipment

1 Boiling container. Some solids need to be

boiled for a while at the start of the winemaking process.

2 Plastic pail — ordinary household ones, dustbins or garbage pails — the fermenting must is first put in this. The pail should be colourless or white. Choose one with a shiny, hard type of surface.

It is useful to have two of these.

A glass fermentation or storage jar with airlock and bung.

3 Fermentation and storage jars. These are used for fermenting the wine and for storing before bottling. They are usually standard glass jars with two lifting rings on the neck.

Although glass jars are the best they may be difficult to obtain owing to shortages, in which case polythene or plastic containers with screw caps can be used. These containers should be new as polythene often retains the smell of its previous contents. If the container is used exclusively for winemaking and sterilized after use it can be used over and over again.

Wooden casks, if properly cleaned, can be used for storage.

4 Airlock. An airlock or fermentation trap is fitted into the neck of the fermentation vessel and prevents air and bacteria from entering and,

at the same time, allows carbon dioxide to escape. Airlocks are available in glass and plastic. The most popular is a U-tube with two bulbs. The U-bend is filled with water sterilized with a Campden tablet or sodium metabisulphite.

Both glass and plastic airlocks have their advantages. The glass lock has the advantage that the water does not readily evaporate, but, on the other hand, it is fragile and not so easy to clean.

Do not immerse plastic airlocks in very hot water or they may soften and lose their shape.

5 Bored rubber bung. The airlock is inserted through the bung and placed in the neck of the fermentation vessel. Bungs, ready bored through the centre, are available for the storage jars.

The bungs are usually made from rubber or cork. Rubber bungs are preferable as they are easier to sterilize and give a better fit, making an airtight seal. The numerous small cracks and crevices in the cork can harbour a multitude of bacteria harmful to winemaking. Also, these cracks can result in incomplete sealing of a container. If liquid is seen leaking from the sides of the cork during fermentation replace the cork immediately.

Make sure that the bungs you buy fit tightly into the neck of the fermentation or storage vessels you use.

6 Plain bungs. These are used to seal the storage jars after the fermentation period.

7 A siphon tube. This is a plastic tube used to transfer wine from one vessel to another placed at a lower level.

One end of the tube is inserted into the top jar and the opposite end is sucked. When the wine is flowing into your mouth this end is placed into the neck of the lower jar. The wine will continue to flow as long as the liquid level of the lower container is lower than that of the upper one.

If this sounds unhygienic to you, a plastic tube fitted with a simple pump at the opposite end is available and is also very convenient for transferring wine when siphoning is not possible. A small plastic tap to fit onto the end of the tube is another useful addition.

8 Bottles. These are needed for bottling the finished wine. Most wine bottles hold $\frac{1}{8}$ of a gallon (76 cl) but 1 litre bottles — and larger sizes — can be acquired. Remember, wines age more quickly in smaller bottles — the larger the bottle the longer the maturation process takes.

Red wines are traditionally stored in brown or green bottles for a good reason — wines change from red to brown if exposed to daylight. If you can keep them in the dark, the colour of the bottles does not matter so much.

For sparkling wines use specially strengthened champagne bottles for reasons mentioned elsewhere.

9 Corks. A supply of corks or plastic stoppers are needed for the wine bottles. Both should be efficiently sterilized before use, especially the corks.

If bottles are only to be filled for a short while, the flanged type of cork is convenient, being easy to withdraw. These can be used over and over again until they lose their good fit.

Plastic stoppers can be used but it is often difficult to get a good fit. And, when they do fit well, they seal so efficiently that they can be very difficult to remove.

By and large it is better to use the longer, straight-sided corks; they usually seal the best and are the most often used.

10 Corking tool. If straight-sided corks are to be used something is needed to bang them in. The simplest instrument for this is a 'flogger'— a heavy shaft of wood with a flat top which is used to 'flog' the cork in. But accidents can happen and the use of a flogger is not recommended.

A selection of wine bottles.

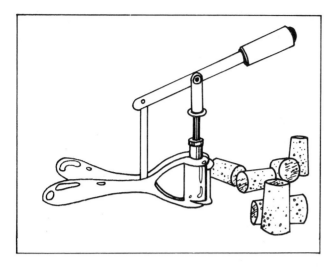

Wine 6
The hydrometer

A hydrometer consists of a weighted glass tube with a bulbous end and a scale along its length. For winemaking the scale goes from .990 to 1.150. Liquid is placed in a trial jar and the hydrometer placed in it. It floats

A corking tool is the easiest to use. There are two or three types available which compress the cork and drive it in with one simple movement.

11 Nylon sieve. This is used to strain the must. Instead, or after, the must can be strained through a nylon filter bag specially made for the purpose. Some types are available complete with frame to hold the bag open, secured to the table edge; otherwise a frame must be constructed at home.

12 Funnel. A plastic funnel, 6 to 9 inches (150 to 230 mm) in diameter is required for filling bottles. It is also used for filtering wines, unless one of the proprietary filters is purchased.

13 Hydrometer. A hydrometer is a most important accessory in winemaking for those not content merely to follow the instructions on the label of concentrates. It measures the amount of sugar present in a solution and tells you whether a must will finish as a dry or sweet wine after fermentation.

In addition it tells you the amount of sugar to be added to the must to give the required alcoholic strength, the potential percentage of alcohol at the commencement of fermentation, and the progress of fermentation — when the hydrometer indicates there is no sugar left the fermentation is over.

Measuring S.G. of finished wine with hydrometer.

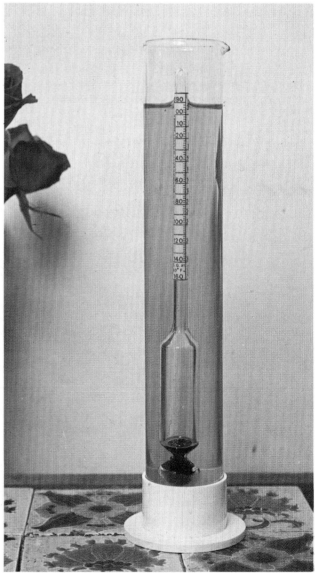

NELSON HARGREAVES

vertically in the liquid, scale uppermost, the reading being observed where the scale cuts through the surface of the liquid. It is usually adjusted to give correct readings for a liquid at a temperature of 60°F (15.6°C) but, for the purposes of winemaking, the readings are sufficiently accurate if the temperature of the liquid varies between 51°F and 69°F (10.6°C and 20.6°C).

How it works

The measurement taken is the specific gravity (S.G.) of the must or wine. (The S.G. of pure water is 1.000 and readings are relative to water.) The more sugar there is dissolved in the wine the denser the wine will be and the higher the hydrometer will float. When the sugar is entirely converted to alcohol, which is less dense that water, the hydrometer will sink down further and read, possibly, .990.

Thus the hydrometer, which is used in a long, narrow 'trial jar', can be used for determining:

1 The S.G. (and hence the sugar content) of the must before fermentation.

2 The amount of sugar to be added to the must to give the required alcoholic strength.

3 The potential percentage of alcohol at the commencement of fermentation.

4 The progress of fermentation.

5 The actual percentage of alcohol at the conclusion of fermentation.

To determine whether a must will produced a dry or sweet wine here is a guide for the reading:

Dry   —1.088 to 1.095
Medium —1.110 to 1.130
Sweet   —1.135 to 1.150

The specific gravities of the actual wine, when fermentation has ceased is:

Dry wine: .085 to .990
Medium wine: .990 to 1.001
Sweet wine: 1.001 to 1.005

The hydrometer and alcohol content

It is sugar that the yeast enzymes convert to alcohol, so the amount of sugar present is related to the alcohol content of the final product. (But do remember that after a certain percentage of alcohol is present in the liquid, about 10% to 17% by volume, the yeast is killed and further fermentation brought to a halt. Any remaining sugar stays unconverted and goes to produce a sweet wine.)

The hydrometer reading of the must suggests the amount of sugar still needed to produce the required alcohol content.

If a hydrometer reading is taken initially a further reading will indicate the progress of fermentation.

The table shows the potential % alcohol that should be obtained for a certain S.G.

For a must of a specific S.G. the amount of sugar already present and the potential % of alcohol is as follows, per gallon (4.5 litres).

S. G.	Sugar already present			Potential % alcohol	S. G.	Sugar already present			Potential % alcohol
	lb	oz	kg			lb	oz	kg	
1.040		13	.36	5.4	1.085	1	15	.879	11.4
1.045		15	.42	6.1	1.090	2	1	.936	12.1
1.050	1	1	.48	6.8	1.095	2	3	.992	12.8
1.055	1	3	.53	7.4	1.100	2	5	1.05	13.4
1.060	1	5	.59	8.1	1.105	2	7	1.11	14.1
1.065	1	7	.65	8.8	1.110	2	9	1.16	14.7
1.070	1	9	.70	9.5	1.115	2	11	1.22	15.4
1.075	1	11	.76	10.1	1.120	2	13	1.28	16.0
1.080	1	13	.82	10.8	1.125	2	15	1.33	16.8

It will be noticed that for every two ounces of sugar added to the must, its S.G. rises by .005 and its potential alcohol by approximately 0.65%. These are useful figures to remember.

Wine 7 Additional equipment

1 Boiler, 2 Filter, 3 Labels, 4 Liquidizer or blender, 5 Measuring jug, 6 Mashers and spoons, 7 Press, 8 Safety lock.

1 Boiler. If you intend to make wine in large quantities and the recipe calls for boiling the pulp a small electric boiler will make life a lot easier and safer; it is difficult for some people to lift five gallons (23 litres) of boiling mash from the top of a cooker.

2 Filter. Sometimes a wine will not clear and needs to be fined or filtered. A number of proprietary filters are available, one incorporating a force pump that enables filtering to be completed in a few minutes. There are also a number of filtering and fining materials that enable wine to be cleared of all cloudiness or haze.

3 Labels. You can add a professional touch to your bottles with some of the many colourful wine labels which are sold in packets. Better still, have your own printed. In any case, even if the label is just plain, all wine you make should be carefully labelled with contents and date of bottling.

4 Liquidizer or blender. A liquidizer or blender is excellent for preparing ingredients for wine must. If you have a lot of fruit to mince (grind) or purée you will find it a slow process with a mincer or a liquidizer of the smallest household type. The larger professional models, that will also slice and grate, are a better investment.

5 Measuring jug. A one litre glass or plastic measuring jug is very useful.

6 Mashers and spoons. These are handy items for breaking down soft ingredients — the ordinary potato masher with slots is ideal, but choose the stainless steel type. Large stainless steel spoons are also useful, but wooden spoons can be used instead if well sterilized before use.

7 Press. A press is a device for extracting the maximum amount of juice from the fruit or pulp. If you make a lot of wine and in large quantities, a press is useful to have provided you have space to store it.

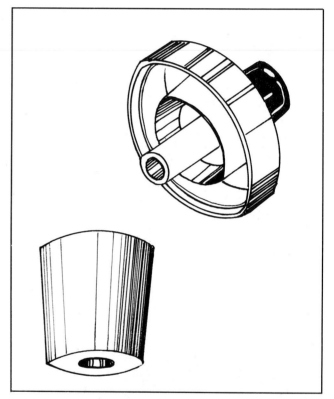

8 Safety lock. The safety lock, or dry fermentation lock, is an excellent device to close the storage container if there is any doubt as to whether or not fermentation has finished completely, and as a precaution in case it restarts.

Two or three types are available to fit 1 gallon (4.5 litre) containers. One sort, using an enclosed steel ball to maintain the seal, has a stem of the same size as an airlock so it can be inserted into a bored rubber bung and then into the container, thus ensuring a better seal than the all-plastic type.

Wine 8 Hygiene

Hygiene is of the utmost importance in wine-making. Fortunately the chemical sodium metabisulphite which is used for sterilization is cheap and easily obtainable. It serves also as an anti-oxidant in the must and as a preservative for finished wine.

Sodium metabisulphite is obtainable in tablet form, known as Campden tablets, or as a powder. The tablets, crushed, are very convenient to add to the must or the finished wine, but a stock solution made from the powder is easier for the sterilization of equipment. Sodium metabisulphite needs an acid medium for effective results.

Sterilizing bottles, corks and corker.

Making a stock solution

To make a stock solution, dissolve $1\frac{1}{2}$ oz (43 g) of the powder with $\frac{1}{8}$ oz (3.5 g) of citric acid in 1 gallon (4.5 litres) of warm water. Caution — do not inhale the fumes.

If, for any reason, sodium metabisulphite powder is difficult to obtain, 7 or 8 crushed Campden tablets equal approximately $\frac{1}{2}$ oz (14 g) of the powder.

Thoroughly rinse or soak everything in the solution: buckets, siphon tube, bottles, etc. Do not rinse them in fresh water but allow everything to drip dry. The same sterilization rules also apply to corks, bungs, stoppers and airlocks. Soak these items well in the solution before use.

If the solution is stored in a closed container it can be used over and over again until the fumes are no longer apparent.

Wooden casks

Wooden casks are not often seen these days, but if you get hold of one and want to use it for storing wine special care care must be taken to thoroughly clean and sterilize it.

First, if it has dried out it must be filled with water to which a quantity of stock solution has been added, and allowed to soak well until the wood has swollen and all leaks have disappeared. Next, empty it out and fill with very hot water to which washing soda or lime has been added. Partly empty it and go over the entire inside with a long stiff brush. Empty it again and if much debris comes away repeat the brushing until it is clean.

When there is no trace of a musty or sour odour coming from the cask it can be considered safe. Rinse it out once or twice more with the sterilizing solution and allow to drain.

Bottles

A good way of cleaning encrusted bottles is with about 3 feet (1 m) of metal chain such as is used for bath plugs. Put a little water in the bottle, drop in most of the chain and swirl it about vigorously. Alternatively use a nylon or bristle brush on a wire handle.

Wine Methods 9

Each recipe gives detailed step by step instructions on how to make wine. However here are the various procedures to give you an idea of the processes.

Preparation of wine musts

If you are using canned grape juice concentrates for your winemaking the work has all been done for you, and this section can be ignored. The next that concerns you is 'Adding the sugar'.

Various methods of must preparation are required according to the ingredients used. The basic principles are given below but any special requirements will be noted in the individual recipes.

Ingredient	Preparation required
Root vegetables	Boil for long enough to soften the material, but do not overcook or the flavour will be lost. Mash and press or place in a liquidizer or blender if preferred.
Berries and soft fruit, except grapes	Pour nearly boiling water over fruit to cover. Leave for two or three days until mushy.
Grapes	Press out the juice; soaking is not required.
Apples, pears	Chop up and soak in cold water for two or three days with one crushed Campden tablet. Press, liquidize or blend.
Canned fruits, fresh stone fruits	Pour nearly boiling water over the fruit to cover.

SCALA

Dried fruits   Remove raisin or sultana seeds, then chop up or mince (grind) before adding to the must.

The juice is not extracted immediately after the above preparation in every instance: sometimes yeast and sugar are added to the pulp which is then allowed to ferment before juice extraction, as set out in individual recipes.

When the pulp is to be fermented in this way it is placed in a container closed to bacteria, flies and wild yeasts, but open to the air. The plastic pail should be covered with a piece of fabric sheeting or 5 to 6 layers of muslin or cheese cloth. Do not use plastic sheeting as this will prevent air getting to the must.

This is called the aerobic fermentation period. After this the must is transferred to a nylon filter bag suspended over a plastic pail for the juice to drain into. Coarse particles may first be removed by passing the pulp through a semi-rigid nylon strainer.

Old Roman mosaic shows grapes being trampled.

Complete extraction may take a day or less, depending on the proportion of juice to solid matter remaining. With some strongly flavoured fruits, such as elderberries or blackcurrants, one or two pints of hot water poured into the bag will flush out more juice, but do not overdo this second process. Except with parsnips, you can squeeze the bag to hasten the process and obtain more juice.

Preparation of mead musts

Honey — the main ingredient of mead — must be sterilized to destroy bacteria and mould spores before fermentation. The only certain way is to add water to the honey and bring the mixture to the boil, but if fruit or juices are to be added, boil the honey first and separately, otherwise unwanted pectin may be extracted from the fruit.

Crushed Campden tablets can be used as an

17

Preparing grapes for pressing. The traditional trampling has been largely abandoned.

alternative to boiling but their action is not so powerful.

Adding the sugar

The next stage is to add the sugar. Most wine-makers seem to follow the practice of adding all the sugar at one time and most of the recipes therefore call for this to be done. However, it is often beneficial to split the sugar into two or even more portions, and add these in stages.

Other additions

Pectin destroying enzymes, available in liquid or powder form, are added, if required, when the must is cool and 24 hours before the addition of the yeast.
The amount to be added depends on the brand, so follow the instructions on the label.

Tannin. Without tannin wines taste insipid. Bilberries, elderberries, grapes, oakleaves, tea and unpeeled pears all have adequately high tannin content for winemaking, but most other substances call for its addition. However, a small quantity makes a big difference as too much can make the wine very astringent. So if you are going to add tannin be cautious at first, adding less rather than more, and refine the quantity next time.
Grape tannin comes in a fine powder or liquid form. Tannin in powder form does not mix easily, so mix into a thin paste first with a small amount of water before adding.

Here is a suggestion for the amounts needed per gallon (4.5 litres) of wine:
For white wines $\frac{1}{16}$ oz (1.75 g) of powder or 2 to 3 drops of liquid.
For red wines $\frac{1}{8}$ oz (3.5 g) of powder or 4 to 6 drops of liquid.

Tea can be used as an alternative to tannin.

18

A teaspoon (5 ml) of strong infused tea per gallon of must is suggested.

Citric acid is usually added for a well balanced flavour when the base ingredient lacks it. Amounts vary from $\frac{1}{4}$ to $\frac{1}{2}$ oz (7 to 14 g) per gallon. The crystals dissolve easily and are stirred into the must.

Tartaric acid is sometimes added instead of citric acid where a harsher flavour is required. Use in the same quantities as tannin.
When potassium salts are present in the wine the tartaric acid and salts combine to form crystals, but these crystals can be easily removed by refrigerating the wine and racking off into a clean container.

Precipitated chalk. Very acid musts, such as those made from rhubarb, can have their acidity reduced by sprinkling $\frac{1}{2}$ oz (14 g) of precipitated chalk into a gallon (4.5 litres) of must before fermentation. More than this quantity will spoil the flavour. As the action of the chalk develops, the wine will fizz considerably; when it has died down fermentation in the usual way may be commenced.

Glycerine is a natural by-product of wine. Its addition in small quantities — $\frac{1}{8}$ fl oz (3.5 ml) per bottle — can enhance a rough wine, reducing harshness and generally improving the flavour.

Campden tablets, sometimes added to the must to prevent unwanted bacterial action and moulds forming, should be added 24 hours before adding the yeast. Use one crushed tablet per gallon (1.45 litres) of must.

Yeast and starter bottles

To start fermentation yeast must be added together with a nutrient.

Quantities. The amount of yeast per gallon (4.5 litres) is usually one tablet, small bottle or packet of wine yeast and about $\frac{1}{8}$ oz (3.5 g) of granulated yeast. For yeast nutrient use $\frac{1}{8}$ oz (3.5 g) per gallon (4.5 litres) or as directed on the label of the container.

Too much yeast causes rapid fermentation, but may leave a yeasty flavour in the finished wine. This 'off' flavour may persist for a few months but usually disappears with time. Too little yeast may take a long time to get going, or may not start at all.

Starter bottle. Granulated yeast usually starts fermentation off almost immediately, but some of the special wine culture yeasts require activating separately in a 'starter bottle' before addition to the must.
To prepare a starter bottle add the yeast, nutrient, 1 oz (28 g) of sugar, a pinch of citric acid and $\frac{1}{4}$ pint (142 ml) of water (or according to the directions supplied with the yeast) at 77°F (25°C) to a small bottle. Shake thoroughly, plug the bottle with cotton wool (absorbent cotton). Keep the bottle warm about 24 hours. When the yeast is working actively add it to the must. A starter bottle will often get a must fermenting when addition of yeast directly to the must will not.

Temperature and yeast action. The correct temperature is most important to the action of the yeast. If the temperature gets too low (under 50°F or 10°C) fermentation will slow down or stop. If it gets too high (over 90°F or 32°C) the yeast will die.
The temperature during the aerobic fermentation period (while the pail is covered with a cloth) should be about 70°F (21°C).
During the anaerobic fermentation period (when the fermentation vessel is sealed with an airlock) the temperature should be about 65°F (18°C).

Fermentation progress

As the yeast starts to work considerable bubbling and frothing occurs. The must will change to a milky colour as the yeast grows. It is a good idea, if the working area is confined, to place a sheet of newspaper around the fermentation container to avoid damage to wallpaper and surroundings.
When the must has been transferred to the fermentation jar keep an eye on the airlock for

the first few days to make sure there is always water present to maintain the trap; evaporation and spillage may necessitate topping up daily. After this initial activity has slowed down the container can be removed to a cooler place, but preferably not below about 62°F (17°C). Fermentation will gradually decrease and, after about four or five weeks, the line of bubbles around the top of the container will have died away completely — if not, wait another few days to make sure that no gas is being given off.

Racking

Dead yeast and perhaps other solid matter (the 'lees') have by now settled at the bottom of the fermentation jar. If left there, an unpleasant

flavour may be imparted to the wine, which it has now become, and so they should be removed. To do this the wine has to be siphoned into a second sterilized container with a siphon tube or pump. You can stand the wine container on a table and set the second container on the floor. Care should be taken that the tube is clear of the sediment.

This process is called racking the wine.

The lower container should be topped up, if necessary, with cooled boiled water as it is preferable to have the minimum of air space remaining.

Crush one Campden tablet per gallon (4.5 litres) of wine and add before sealing the container with a solid bung or safety lock; these tablets act as a preservative and help to stop further fermentation.

Store in a cool, dry place.

Rack off the wine into a clean container every eight weeks or so, to remove sediment till the wine becomes clear.

Bottling

When the wine has become clear, and then only, it is ready to be bottled. Do not be disappointed if the flavour of the wine at this time does not meet your expectations; it may taste 'yeasty'. The flavour and aroma will improve as the wine is stored — two months for some wines, two years for others.

If the wine does not clear it will need to be fined or filtered.

For each gallon of wine you will need six sterilized bottles and corks. Siphon or pump the wine into them until full, then fit corks or stoppers according to your chosen method. And don't forget to label the bottles before putting them away.

Most winemakers also find it useful to keep a record of their activities — the ingredients of the must, the type of yeast used, the quantity of sugar and when added, other additives, S.G. at various stages and comments on the end results. Such information is very useful for guidance in another year and essential if you want to improve your winemaking.

Racking wine into bottles.

Wine 10 Maximum strength & other wines

Maximum strength wines

To produce wines with an alcohol content above 13%, ever increasing care and nursing is required. Although the activity of most yeasts is inhibited at around 17% alcohol, wines of up to 21% can be produced.

These are the points to watch:

1 Prepare a must with a high fruit content by doubling the quantity of the recipe.

2 Use the correct wine culture yeast — both the Sherry and Tokay types are recommended for high alcoholic strength wines.

3 Maintain the supply of yeast nutrient and vitamins when adding sugar.

4 Keep the temperature correct — 70°F (21°C), or as specified by the directions supplied with the particular yeast.

5 Keep the temperature constant — a thermostatically controlled heater, inserted in the fermentation jar, is available for this purpose.

6 Feed the sugar in gradually, in perhaps six or seven portions, instead of two or three.

Sparkling wines

Sparkling wines are produced by inducing a secondary fermentation within a sealed bottle. This is an advanced process and a first requirement is a number of proper champagne bottles which are specially strengthened — ordinary bottles are not strong enough to withstand the gas pressure developed within. Burst bottles are dangerous! And a word of warning — accidents can still happen.

The true champagne method is lengthy,

requiring at least a year of skilled attention to each bottle, and is unlikely to appeal to the amateur. However, it is possible to make a sparkling wine — that is a wine that is still fermenting slightly, therefore still giving off carbon dioxide gas from the yeast. The French call this state 'petillanté'.

Select a light coloured white wine. Before fermentation has quite finished, rack the wine, but allow a little sediment to rise. Then pour into champagne bottles, leaving room for a syrup made of 2 oz (57 g) of sugar in each bottle. After adding the sugar close securely and wire down the stoppers—the plastic stoppers are best here.

Stand the bottles upright in a warm place (70°F, 21°C), watching them carefully. When a new fermentation is seen to start remove the bottles to cooler surroundings of about 60°F (15.5°C), and leave them for at least nine months.

Open and pour very carefully to avoid disturbing the sediment.

Liqueurs

To make liqueur, use a wine without a strong flavour, since a flavouring agent is added. To fortify the wine a flavourless spirit is required — Polish Vodka, Vybora, is commonly added; this Vodka is obtainable in 100° and 140° proof spirit strengths. Quantities are given below for both strengths.

Having chosen the flavour required, put $\frac{1}{8}$ fl oz (3.5 ml) of the liqueur essence into an ordinary wine bottle, then add 6 oz (170 g) of sugar dissolved in a little hot water. Add the Vodka according to the table below, then fill with the wine; cork securely. No fermentation is involved and the liqueur will be ready in a few days.

Vodka added per bottle				Resultant
100° proof		140° proof		liqueur strength
fl oz	ml	fl oz	ml	proof
3	85	2	56	40°
6	170	4	114	50°
9	256	5	142	60°

Instant wines

So-called 'instant' wines, ready for drinking within a few weeks of starting fermentation, can be produced by the use of concentrates or other light-bodied basic materials, reducing the sugar content, using granulated, quick-acting yeast, and repeated filtering. Such wines will have a low alcoholic content, say 7° to 8°, but are pleasant drinks in the warmer weather. They will not keep for long.

Wine 11 Fining & filtering

If the wine does not clear about two months after the initial racking (or longer if indicated in the recipe), it can be cleared either by fining of filtering. Filtering is usually tried first and if that fails it should be fined. However, some people prefer the Bentonite fining powder to any other method.

Filtering

The filtering agents that may be used are proprietary filters, cellulose powder and

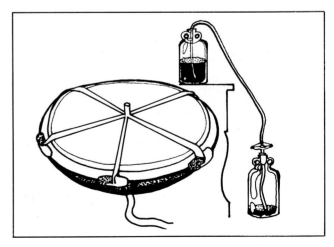

diatomaceous silica.

It should be noted that there is some doubt about the advisability of using asbestos powder (although it is still available in some areas) for reasons of health.

The proprietary filters are efficient and very simple to use. Full instructions are supplied with the filter.

For all other methods you will need a plastic funnel about 6 to 9 inches in diameter (150 to 230 mm), some good quality cotton wool (absorbent cotton), and a support for the funnel. (The support can easily be made from a 12 inch (300 mm) square of hardboard with a 4 inch (100 mm) hole cut in the centre, with both sides covered in thin self-adhesive plastic sheeting for easy cleaning.

Plug the stem of the funnel with cotton wool, packing it down fairly tightly. Sprinkle in a layer of loose-packed cellulose powder or diatomaceous silica, about $\frac{3}{4}$ inch (20 mm) deep. Fill the funnel with wine. At first the powder will tend to float but will gradually settle down. If the wine does not clear pass this first quantity back through the funnel, pouring the wine gently down the side of the funnel so that the filter layer is disturbed as little as possible. If the wine clears proceed to filter the rest. If it does not clear the wine will have to be fined. After a gallon (4.5 litres) has passed through, or if the filtering rate has become too slow, renew the cotton wool and filter medium.

Fining

If filtering does not clear the wine it will have to be fined. The fining agents that may be used are isinglass, egg white, egg shell, proprietary finings or Bentonite.

It is easier to fine wine when it is in bulk rather than in a bottle.

First rack off the wine if there is any sediment into a clean jar.

After initial preparation of the chosen fining ingredients (see below) the fining agent is added to the wine, left from four to six days to clear

Wine being filtered to remove suspended particles in the wine.

the wine, then the wine is carefully racked off into a clean jar or bottles, taking care not to disturb the sediment.

Eggshells. Clean them and bake in an oven until brittle. Crush them into a coarse powder. Sprinkle into the wine, using ½ oz (14 g) to each gallon (4.5 litres).

Egg white. Discard the yolk, pour off up to a pint of the wine and beat the white into this wine — an electric mixer is helpful.
Add the mixture to the bulk of the wine. One egg white will fine 5 gallons (23 litres).

Isinglass and proprietary finings. Pour in a measured quantity, about ½ fl oz (14 ml) per gallon (4.5 litres) or as directed on the label, and stir thoroughly.

Bentonite powder is a fine clay powder which swells in water forming sticky particles which appear to absorb all the haze and cloudiness as they sink to the bottom. It is strongly recommended as a cleaning agent and usually succeeds where some of the other agents only do half the job.
Add ¾ oz (21 g) of the Bentonite powder to ¾ pint (426 ml) of cold water in a pint (568 ml) size bottle. Shake the bottle really vigorously until all the powder has gone into suspension and there is none left sticking to the sides or bottom. Stand the bottle for about a day, shaking occasionally, and it will be found that the powder no longer tends to settle.
It can now be added to the wine — about ¼ fl oz (7 ml) to a bottle or 1 to 1½ fl oz (28 to 42 ml) per gallon (4.5 litres) of wine.
Agitate the wine several times during the first day, then leave it for five or six days, when it should be perfectly clear. Decant or rack the wine carefully, as the sediment is very light.
Bentonite gel is also available. This can be added directly to the wine and merely stirred a few times to disperse it; racking should follow in a few days. Add 8 oz (227 g) per gallon (4.5 litres) of wine.
Note. Do not add more Bentonite than stated above or it may spoil the flavour of the wine — the correct amount will not affect it.

24

Wine 12 Controlling the sugar

Each recipe suggests quantities of sugar to be added and the resulting type of wine — dry, sweet, medium. If you want to adjust this to your own taste, making a wine sweeter or drier, it is advisable to add the sugar in stages and to use a hydrometer. Apart from this, the procedure for making the wine is the same as the recipe.
One way of making medium to sweet wines is to first make a dry one and then, after fermentation has stopped, to add sugar to your taste.

Grape juice concentrates

Many grape juice concentrate recipes call for only 6 pints (3.5 litres) of water initially, with sugar to be added later in two stages, within a certain number of days or when a certain S.G. is reached. If you do not want to bother with a hydrometer follow the recipe and you should finish up with a dry wine of between 10% and 12% alcohol, which is the usual range for a table wine.

Why work with a hydrometer?

Adding the sugar in stages and using a hydrometer has the following advantages:
1 You can calculate the sugar content of the must before adding any sugar.
2 You can calculate more accurately the amount of sugar to be added so controlling the final outcome.
3 If there is too much sugar the yeast is apparently overwhelmed and will not become active. By adding sugar in stages, fermentation is more likely to be complete.
4 You can check the progress of fermentation

and stop adding sugar if yeast activity stops.
5 You can calculate the potential alcohol content at the commencement of fermentation and the actual content at the end of the process. The section on the hydrometer has a table at the end which gives the sugar requirements for the must of a dry, medium and sweet wine and also the final sugar content (S.G.) of the finished wine.

Calculating the sugar needed

Having made a gallon of must, measure its S.G. before adding any sugar. Let us say it is 1.050. Then decide upon the alcohol content that you require; 12% is a good target figure. (It is not advisable to try to increase the alcohol content above this figure or the result may just be a sweeter wine. The aim in winemaking is to make a pleasant beverage.

Refer to the S.G. table and it will be seen that 12% alcohol requires 2lb 1oz (938 g) sugar and that a S.G. of 1.050 represents 1lb 1oz (468 g) of sugar, leaving 16oz (450g) to be added.

These figures are for a dry wine, and will need to be adjusted for sweeter results.

Starting fermentation

This sugar should not be added all at once; indeed, if the S.G. reading is over 1.080 and your aim is a dry wine no more should be added at this stage. For a medium wine you could start at 1.085 and for a sweeter one at 1.090. However, remember the total quantity required as it will be added later when the S.G. has dropped.

Leave space for the sugar to be added in the fermentation vessel, 16oz (450g) of sugar needs a pint of water in which to dissolve easily so it is best not to fill a gallon (4.5 litre) container with more than 6 pints (say 3.5 litres) of must initially. Any topping up can be done with must put aside in a sealed container (preferably refrigerated) or with water.

Adding more sugar

The yeast starts off with considerable bubbling and frothing which slows down after four to five days. After about ten days the S.G. should stand at around 1.010.

An addition of half the sugar, dissolved in a small quantity of hot water, can now be made. Fermentation activity will recommence, but not to such a great extent as before.

After a further five days the hydrometer should read about 1.002 and this is the time to add the final quantity of sugar, in syrup form as before.

From now on fermentation will gradually decrease and after four or five weeks the line of bubbles around the top of the container will have died away completely — if not, wait another few days to make sure that no gas is being given off. The hydrometer should now read .990 (in the example given above), up to 1.001 for a medium wine and up to 1.005 for a sweet wine.

Medium to sweet wines

If the wine needs to be sweeter for your taste, you can add more sugar now.

In case fermentation should restart with the addition of this sugar wait a few days to make sure it has completely stopped before racking and sealing.

Actual alcohol present

For an approximate calculation of the actual alcohol content of your finished wine here is a simple formula.

Subtract the S.G. of the wine when fermentation ends (say.990) from the original total S.G. calculation (1.090, for a day wine with 12% alcohol) disregard the decimal point and divide by 8.2.

$$1090 - 990 = \frac{100}{8.2} = 12.2\% \text{ alcohol.}$$

Wine 13 Storing decanting & serving

Storing

Wine is best stored in a cool, well ventilated, dark, dry place with a temperature of 45° to 50°F (7° to 10°C). If straight-sided corks are used and the bottles are stored for longer than two to three weeks, the bottles must be kept on their sides so that the cork remains wet and swelled to maintain a seal. You will also need a rack or racks in which to stack the bottles. Plastic stoppered bottles can be stood upright. Remember, keep the red wines in brown or green bottles and sparkling wines in champagne bottles.

The period before the wine is ready to drink varies widely and can be between six to eight weeks for the concentrates, six to nine months or longer for the fruit and vegetable wines, and even longer — one to two years — for honey based wines such as mead and melomel. However, some 'instant wines' — for which special recipes are given — can be ready within a few weeks of starting.

The period taken from the commencement of storage until the wine is ready for drinking varies according to the main ingredients, the yeast, the temperature and other factors. There is no doubt, however, that as soon as a wine has stopped fermenting it may not taste very pleasant. But as it stands it will gradually become smoother and more mellow.

Wine bottles stacked on their sides for maturing.

FOOD FROM FRANCE

The only sure way to find out if a wine is ready is to taste it, but remember that all wines (except the 'instant' ones) improve with keeping.

Bulk storage and casks

If your wine is stored in a large container the container should be emptied within a week of opening otherwise the wine may turn sour. If you store wine in a wooden cask note that wine drawn off must be replaced reasonably soon or else part of the cask will dry out, also the wine may turn sour.

Any cask not in use should always be stored filled with a sodium metabisulphite solution to prevent the cask from drying out.

Decanting and serving

When the wine is taken from store note if it has any sediment; there is usually a little. If so it should be decanted. Decanting means to pour off the clear wine without disturbing the sediment — this is not difficult if the bottle is emptied at one steady pouring and is not tipped too high, thus avoiding 'glugging' as it pours. The wine can be served from a clean bottle or poured into a jug.

White and rosé wines are normally served chilled. This does not mean refrigerated for several hours! If the wine is too cold the bouquet is lost. Red wines are served at room temperature.

Wine 14 Trouble~shooting faults & remedies

FAULT	CAUSE	REMEDY
Must will not ferment	Too cold	Raise temperature to at least 70°F (21°C).
	Excess of sugar	If a hydrometer reading of must is above 1.090, halve the must and top up each half with water. Start again as if with a fresh must.
	Yeast added too soon after Campden tablets or depectinizer	If Campden tablets or depectinizes are added to a must, 24 hours should elapse before adding yeast. Wait, then add more yeast.
Fermentation stops too soon, and wine too sweet	Too cold or	Raise temperature.
	Yeast action inhibited by high alcohol content or	Try mixing fresh yeast in a starter bottle. Add this to one pint (568 ml) of the wine. When fermentation restarts, add the rest of the wine, one pint (568 ml) at a time, waiting for fermentation to continue before adding the next quantity. If this fails, use the wine for Sangria, wine cups etc, or blend with a very dry wine.
	Yeast action inhibited by too much initial sugar. Lack of yeast nutrient or acid	Try as above, adding yeast nutrient and acid. Alternatively double the quantity of water and start again.

REMEDY	CAUSE	FAULT
Yeast flavour	Probably use of excessive yeast	Leave in storage for two or three more months—it will slowly cure itself.
Other 'off' flavours	Too long between racking leaving lees in wine	Rack when fermentation is finished and thereafter every eight weeks or as sediment forms.
Wine turns into vinegar	Vinegar fly or bacteria has got into wine	None—discard it. Use sound fruit. Always keep the fermentation vessel covered during the aerobic fermentation period and sealed with an airlock while fermenting. Try adding Campden tablets with the must and for storage.
Fermentation restarts, or will not stop	Yeast not worked out	Add Campden tablets to inhibit yeast action. White wines are prone to restarting fermentation in hot weather.
Crystal formation	Tartaric acid reacting with potassium salts	Refrigerate the wine and rack into a clean container, leaving crystals behind.
Wine is hazy	Pectin haze, pectin destroying enzyme not used	For fruit high in pectin a pectin destroying enzyme should be added before fermentation.
	Starch haze caused by unripe fruit or cereal	These hazes are not always completely removable, but filtering or fining usually cleans them. Always use a cereal yeast for cereal wines.
	Suspended particles in the wine	In general suspended particles can be filtered out.
Insipid wine	Insufficient acid or tannin	Blend with a stronger wine, especially one that is too harsh or acid.
Oiliness or ropiness	The work of lactic acid bacteria	Wine takes on appearance of egg white and goes thick. Beat up wine into a froth and add two Campden tablets per gallon, the taste is not affected.
Moulds	The work of micro-organisms	Caused sometimes when fermentation is slow in starting or utensils not properly sterilized. Skim off mould and add a Campden tablet. After 24 hours add more yeast.

All these faults can be avoided by sterilization, the proper adjustment of additives, the use of Campden tablets to suppress undesirable bacteria and wild yeasts, and the addition of a wine yeast starter in a vigorously fermenting condition.

Wine 15 Recipes A to Z

The recipes that follow have been chosen mainly on the grounds of practicality and availability of the ingredients, but they also afford an opportunity to try some of the more unusual wines.

These recipes must not be considered as hard and fast rules; if the recipe calls for $3\frac{1}{2}$lb (1.59 kg) of sugar and you find that 3lb (1.36 kg) suits your taste better, then use 3lb (1.36 kg). Similarly, if you dislike astringency in wines, do not add any tannin. If they are too acid, cut down the citric acid or lemon juice.

The quantities given all assume that 1 gallon (4.5 litres) of wine is being made; if you want to make 2 or 5 gallons (9 or 23 litres) then just double everything or multiply everything by 5, respectively. If the must is short of the quantity required to fill the fermentation jar, make it up with warm water.

Sugar and the hydrometer

The type of wine (dry, medium or sweet) that you should obtain by exactly following the recipe is stated. If you wish to vary the sweetness (or dryness), it is best to use a hydrometer and add enough sugar, initially, to give an S.G. of 1.080 for a dry wine, 1.085 for a medium one and 1.090 for a sweeter one, following the instructions given elsewhere in this book.

Quantities

Flower petals and leaves are measured by liquid measure, using the gallon or pint markings on a container. The measures given in the recipe assume the petals or leaves to be lightly pressed down.

Washing

In these days of selective weedkillers and garden sprays, some of which are poisonous to man, always wash fruit, leaves and plants thoroughly before starting to make the wine. However, do not wash fruit until you are ready to start making the must as washed fruit deteriorates very rapidly in hot weather.

Temperature

The temperature during the aerobic fermentation period (when fermentation is occurring while the pail is covered with a cloth) should be about 70°F (21°C).

During the anaerobic fermentation period (when the fermentation vessel is sealed with an airlock) the temperature should be about 65°F (18°C).

Almond & raisin wine

Classification: Dessert, Sweet, White

INGREDIENTS	UK/US	METRIC
Almonds	2oz	57g
Raisins	1lb	454g
Lemons, 3		
Sugar, light brown	3lb	1.36kg
Tannin,		
2 to 3 drops or	$\frac{1}{16}$oz	1.75g
Yeast, all-purpose		
Yeast nutrient		
Campden tablets		

1 Blanch (skin) the almonds by soaking in very hot water for a few minutes.
2 Pare the zest from the lemons and squeeze out the juice.
3 Chop the almonds and raisins, deseeding if necessary. Simmer in 1 gallon (4.5 litres) of water for one hour.
4 Strain into a pail and make up the liquid

to 1 gallon (4.5 litres).

5 Add the sugar and stir until dissolved; then add the lemon zest and juice, the tannin, yeast and the yeast nutrient.

6 Cover the pail and stand it in a warm place for 14 days, stirring daily.

7 At the end of this period, strain into a fermentation vessel and insert an airlock.

8 When fermentation is complete, rack the wine into a clean container, add one crushed Campden tablet and close with a bung or safety lock.

9 Rack every two months till clear.

Apple & bilberry wine

Classification: Dessert, Sweet, Red

INGREDIENTS	UK/US	METRIC
Apples, ripe	6lb	2.7kg
Bilberries	4lb	1.8kg
Raisins	8oz	227g
Sugar	3½lb	1.59kg
Citric acid	¼oz	7g
Yeast, all-purpose		
Yeast nutrient		
Campden tablets		
Pectin destroying enzyme		

1 Inspect the apples, cut out any bruised parts and remove the pips.

2 Put them in a pail with ½ gallon (2.3 litres) of cold water and two crushed Campden tablets; stir together.

3 Stir and mash the apples each day for a week, then strain.

4 Three days after preparing the apples, put the bilberries into a second pail and cover

30

with ½ gallon (2.3 litres) of hot water. Leave for three days, then add the pectin destroying enzyme.

5 After a further 24 hours, thoroughly squeeze out the must and strain it.

6 Mix the two fruit juices together in a third pail, chop up and add the raisins (deseeding if necessary) and add the sugar, citric acid, yeast and yeast nutrient.

7 Stir until the sugar has dissolved, then cover the pail and stand it in a warm place, stirring daily.

8 After two to three weeks, strain into a fermentation vessel and fit an airlock.

9 When fermentation is complete, rack off into a clean container, add one crushed Campden tablet and close with a bung or safety lock.

10 Rack every two months till clear.

Apricot (canned) wine

Classification: Table, Medium, White

1 Proceed exactly as for Peach (canned) Wine, substituting 2lb (907kg) canned apricot halves or pulp for the peaches.

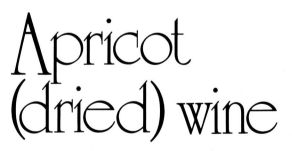

Apricot (dried) wine

Classification: Dessert, Sweet, Golden

INGREDIENTS	UK/US	METRIC
Dried apricots	1lb	454g
Raisins	1lb	454g
Sugar, light brown	3lb	1.36kg
Citric acid	¼oz	7g

Tannin,
2 to 3 drops or $\frac{1}{16}$oz 1.75g
Yeast, all-purpose
Yeast nutrient
Campden tablets
Pectin destroying
enzyme

1 Wash the apricots, cut them up and soak them for 12 hours in enough cold water to cover the fruit.
2 Chop the raisins and deseed if necessary. Place them, with the apricots and the water in which they have soaked, into a pail.
3 Dissolve the sugar in a little hot water and add this to the pail, together with the pectin destroying enzyme.
4 Add the tannin and citric acid and stir thoroughly, then add enough hot water to make up to 1 gallon (4.5 litres).
5 After 24 hours, add the yeast and yeast nutrient.
6 Cover the pail and stand it in a warm place.
7 Leave to ferment for eight days, stirring daily.
8 Strain the must into a fermentation vessel and seal with an airlock.
9 When fermentation is complete, rack into a clean container, add one crushed Campden tablet and close with a bung or safety lock.
10 Rack every two months till clear.

Comment
This wine is an excellent basis for Apricot liqueur.

Apricot (fresh) wine

Classification: Table, Medium, Golden

INGREDIENTS	UK/US	METRIC
Apricots, ripe and sweet	4lb	1.8kg
Sugar	3lb	1.36kg
Citric acid	$\frac{1}{4}$oz	7g
Tannin, 2 or 3 drops or	$\frac{1}{16}$oz	1.75g
Yeast, all-purpose		
Yeast nutrient		
Campden tablets		
Pectin destroying enzyme		

1 Wash the apricots well and allow them to drain.
2 Put the apricots into a pan and boil with $1\frac{1}{4}$ gallons (5.7 litres) of water.
3 Take out the stones, crack 12 stones and remove the kernels. Add the kernels to the pan and boil for another 10 minutes.
4 Strain the liquid into a pail; add the sugar, citric acid, tannin and pectin destroying enzyme. Stir well until the sugar has dissolved, leave for 24 hours.
5 Add the yeast and nutrient, cover the pail and stand it in a warm place. Stir daily.
6 After three days, strain the must into a fermentation jar and seal it with an airlock.
7 When fermentation is complete, rack the wine into a container, add one crushed Campden tablet, and close with a bung or safety lock.
8 Rack every two months, for six months, then less frequently as sediment forms.

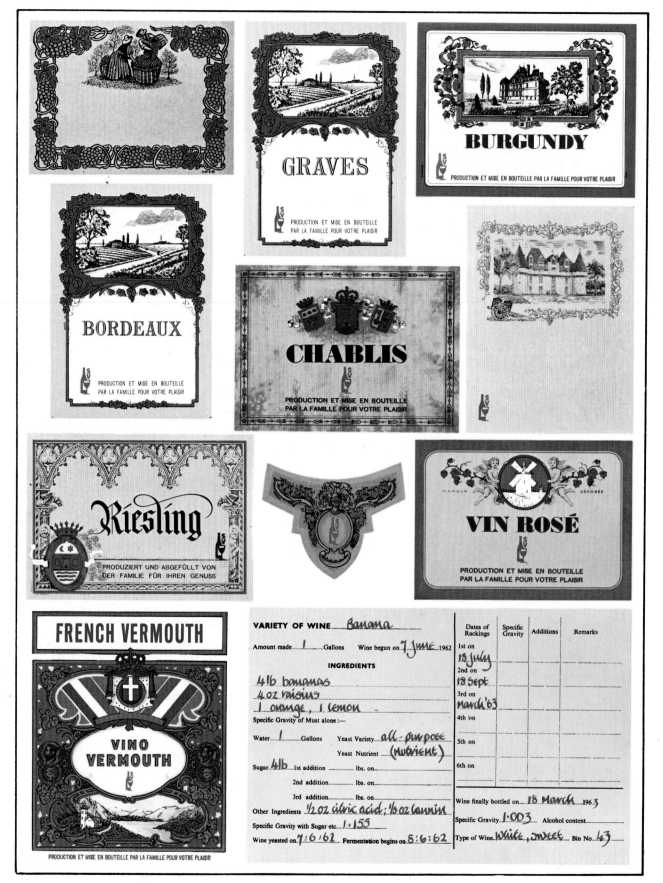

Banana wine

Classification: Dessert, Sweet, White

INGREDIENTS	UK/US	METRIC
Bananas, old and very ripe	4lb	1.8kg
Raisins	4oz	113g
Orange, 1		
Lemon, 1		
Sugar	3lb	1.36kg
Citric acid	$\frac{1}{2}$oz	14g
Tannin, 4 to 6 drops or	$\frac{1}{8}$oz	3.5g
Yeast, all-purpose		
Yeast nutrient		
Campden tablets		

1 Peel the bananas, retaining about $\frac{1}{2}$lb (227g) of their skins.
2 Put the bananas and skins in a muslin (or cheesecloth) bag, place it in a large pan or boiler with $1\frac{1}{4}$ gallons (5.7 litres) of water and simmer for half hour.
3 Squeeze the juice from the orange and lemon.
4 Place the sugar, orange and lemon juice, chopped deseeded raisins, tannin and citric acid in a pail.
5 Pour the liquid from the bananas into the pail, and stir until the sugar is fully dissolved.
6 When cool, squeeze as much juice as possible from the bag into the pail.
7 Add the yeast and yeast nutrient.
8 Cover the pail and stand it in a warm place for seven days, stirring daily.
9 Strain off the juice into a fermentation vessel, and close it with an airlock.
10 When fermentation is complete, rack into a clean container, add one crushed Campden tablet and close with a bung or safety lock.
11 Rack every two months till clear.

A selection of labels for homemade wines and a page from a wine log book. Don't forget to write the date of bottling on the label.

Barley & raisin wine

Classification: Table, Medium, White

INGREDIENTS	UK/US	METRIC
Whole barley grains	1lb	454g
Raisins	1lb	454g
Potatoes	1lb	454g
Sugar	$3\frac{1}{2}$lb	1.59kg
Citric acid	$\frac{1}{2}$oz	14g
Tannin,		
2 to 3 drops or	$\frac{1}{16}$oz	1.75g
Yeast, cereal-type		
Yeast nutrient		
Campden tablets		

1 Soak the barley in water overnight.
2 Peel and chop up the potatoes.
3 Deseed the raisins if necessary, mix them with the barley and put the mixture through a mincer or grinder.
4 Put the chopped potatoes, minced barley and raisins, and sugar into a pail.
5 Heat almost to boiling point sufficient water to cover the contents of the pail, and pour it in.
6 Add the citric acid and tannin.
7 Add one crushed Campden tablet, then cover the pail.
8 After 24 hours, add the yeast and nutrient, and place the pail in a warm place to ferment.
9 Leave for 10 days, stirring daily.
10 Strain the liquid into a fermentation vessel, make it up to 1 gallon (4.5 litres) and fit an airlock.
11 When fermentation is complete, rack into a clean container, add one crushed Campden tablet and close the container with a bung or safety lock.
12 Rack every two months till clear.

Comment
An easily made wine, needing no boiling or mashing, which usually clears very quickly.

Barley is often used in winemaking. Here are various forms of available barley: whole grains, flaked and ground barley, Ground barley is used in the Greengage Wine recipe. A cereal yeast is recommended when fermenting barley.

DON LAST

Beetroot (beet) wine

Classification: Table, Medium, Red

INGREDIENTS	UK/US	METRIC
Beetroot (beet)	4lb	1.8kg
Lemon, 1		
Ginger root, 1 piece		
Sugar	3½lb	1.59kg
Citric acid	½oz	14g
Tannin,		
4 to 6 drops or	⅛oz	3.5g
Yeast, all-purpose		
Yeast nutrient		
Campden tablets		

1 Wash the beetroot; do not skin.
2 Slice the beetroot into 1 gallon (4.5 litres) of water and simmer it until the vegetable is tender.
3 Squeeze the juice from the lemon, and 'bruise' the ginger.
4 Strain the liquid from the beetroot into a pail; add the lemon juice, the piece of ginger, the sugar, the citric acid and the tannin; stir until the sugar has dissolved.
5 Add hot water to make the volume up to 1 gallon (4.5 litres), then add the yeast and the nutrient.
6 Cover the pail and stand it in a warm place for three days, stirring daily.
7 Strain off the juice into a fermentation vessel and close it with an airlock.
8 When fermentation is complete, rack into a clean container, add one crushed Campden tablet and close with a bung or safety lock.
9 Rack every two months till clear.

Comment
Keep this wine in the dark as much as possible or the wine will turn brown instead of remaining a bright red.

Bilberry (canned) wine

Classification: Table, Medium dry, Red

INGREDIENTS	UK/US	METRIC
Bilberries	2lb	907g
Sugar	2½lb	1.13kg
Citric acid	¼oz	7g
Yeast, all-purpose		
Yeast nutrient		
Campden tablets		
Pectin destroying enzyme		

1 Proceed as for Peach (canned) Wine except that, as there is tannin already present in bilberries, additional tannin need not be added.

Bilberry & raisin (dried) wine

Classification: Dessert, Sweet, Red

INGREDIENTS	UK/US	METRIC
Dried bilberries	1lb	454g
Raisins	1lb	454g
Lemons, 3		
Sugar	3lb	1.36kg
Yeast, all-purpose		
Yeast nutrient		
Campden tablets		

**Pectin destroying
enzyme**

1 Thoroughly wash the bilberries.
2 Soak them in 2 pints (1.14 litres) of hot water for 12 hours, keeping the pail covered.
3 Dissolve half of the sugar in 3 pints (1.7 litres) of hot water; when cool, add this to the bilberries.
4 Chop and deseed the raisins and add these to the pail, then fill it to 1 gallon (4.5 litres) with hot water.
5 Pare the zest from the lemons, squeeze the juice from them and add to the pail, with the remainder of the sugar and the pectin destroying enzyme.
6 Stir well until the sugar has dissolved, then, after 24 hours, add the yeast and nutrient.
7 Cover the pail and stand it in a warm place for seven days, stirring daily.
8 Strain juice into a fermentation vessel and seal with an airlock.
9 When fermentation is complete, rack the must into a clean container, add one crushed Campden tablet and close it with a bung or safety lock.
10 Rack every two months till clear.

Bilberry (fresh) wine

Classification: Table, Dry, Red
1 Make as for Blueberry wine, substituting 2lb (907g) bilberries.

Comment
In Scotland, bilberries are called blaeberries, and another local name is whortle berry.

Birch sap & pear wine

Classification: Table, Medium, White

INGREDIENTS	UK/US	METRIC
Birch sap	6 pints	3.4 litres
Pears, ripe	12 oz	340g
Sultanas (or white raisins)	8oz	227g
Sugar	3lb	1.36kg
Citric acid	$\frac{1}{2}$oz	14g
Tannin, 2 to 3 drops or	$\frac{1}{16}$oz	1.75g
Yeast, all-purpose		
Yeast nutrient		
Campden tablets		

1 Deseed and chop up the sultanas.
2 Peel the pears and cut them into small pieces, removing the pips.
3 Put the pears into a pan, add a crushed Campden tablet and water to cover.
Bring to the boil, then simmer for 15 minutes.
Add the sap, bring to the boil and remove from heat.
4 Put the sultanas into a pail and pour in the sap and pear mixture.
5 Add the citric acid and tannin and stir well.
6 Dissolve the sugar in a little hot water and pour this into the pail.
7 Add the yeast and nutrient, stir and cover. Stand it in a warm place for five days, stirring daily.
8 Strain into a fermentation vessel, make it up to 1 gallon (4.5 litres) of must with warm water and fit an airlock.
9 When fermentation is complete, rack the wine into a clean container, add one crushed Campden tablet and close it with a bung or safety lock.
10 Rack every two months, for six months, then at longer intervals as sediment forms.

 Blackberry wine

Classification: Dessert, Sweet, Red

INGREDIENTS	UK/US	METRIC
Blackberries	4lb	1.8kg
Lemon, 1		
Sugar, light brown	3lb	1.36kg
Citric acid	$\frac{1}{4}$oz	7g
Tannin,		
4 to 6 drops or	$\frac{1}{8}$oz	3.5g
Yeast, all-purpose*		
Yeast nutrient		
Campden tablets		
Pectin destroying enzyme		

1 Wash the berries, and allow them to drain.
2 Soak the berries, with a crushed Campden tablet, in cold water; this will bring out any worms. Remove them! Rinse the fruit and drain.
3 Pare the zest from the lemon, and squeeze out the juice.
4 Put the berries, lemon juice, rind, citric acid and tannin into a pail, and pour 1 gallon (4.5 litres) of boiling water over them, to cover. Crush the fruit with the back of a large spoon.
5 Cover the pail and allow it to stand for two days, stirring daily.
6 Add the pectin destroying enzyme and leave for a further 24 hours.
7 Dissolve the sugar in a little hot water.
8 Strain the juice from the berries into a second pail and add the sugar syrup, yeast and nutrient.
9 Cover the pail and stand it in a warm place for three days, stirring daily.
10 Strain into a fermentation vessel, and fit an airlock.
11 When fermentation is complete, rack into a clean container, add one crushed Campden tablet and seal the fermentation vessel with a bung or safety lock.
12 Rack every two months, till clear.

Comment
*Burgundy-type cultured yeast can be used as an alternative.

 Blackcurrant wine

Classification: Dessert, Sweet, Red

INGREDIENTS	UK/US	METRIC
Blackcurrants	4lb	1.8kg
Sugar	$3\frac{1}{2}$lb	1.59kg
Citric acid	$\frac{1}{4}$oz	7g
Yeast, all-purpose		
Yeast nutrient		
Campden tablets		
Pectin destroying enzyme		

1 Wash the currants carefully and remove the stems.
2 Put the currants and 1 gallon (4.5 litres) of water into a pan and bring to the boil, then simmer for 20 minutes.
3 Strain the liquid into a pail.
4 Add the sugar and stir until the sugar is dissolved.
5 When lukewarm, add the citric acid and pectin destroying enzyme.
6 Cover the pail, then stand it in a warm place.
7 After 24 hours, add the yeast and nutrient.
8 After 14 days, strain the must into a fermentation jar and seal it with an airlock.
9 When fermentation has finished, rack the wine into a clean container, add one crushed Campden tablet and close the container with a bung or safety lock.
10 Rack every two months, for six months, then at longer intervals as sediment forms.

Blueberry wine

Classification: Table, Dry, Red

INGREDIENTS	UK/US	METRIC
Blueberries (fresh)	2lb	907g
Sugar	2lb	907g
Citric acid	¼oz	7g
Yeast, all-purpose		
Yeast nutrient		
Campden tablets		
Pectin destroying enzyme		

1 Wash and drain the berries.
2 Put the berries into a pail and pour ½ gallon (2.3 litres) of boiling water over them.
3 Stir in the sugar and citric acid, then add a further ½ gallon (2.3 litres) of very hot water and stir until the sugar has dissolved.
4 When the must is lukewarm, add the pectin destroying enzyme.
5 After 24 hours, add the yeast and nutrient.
6 Cover the pail and stand it in a warm place for four to five days, stirring daily.
7 Strain the must into a fermentation vessel and close it with an airlock.
8 When fermentation is complete, rack into a clean container, add one crushed Campden tablet and close it with a bung or safety lock.
9 Rack every two months.

Burgundy wine

Classification: Table, Dry, Red

INGREDIENTS	UK/US	METRIC
Burgundy grape juice concentrate, 1 can	2lb 3oz	1kg
Sugar	10oz	284g
Yeast, all-purpose*		
Yeast nutrient		
Campden tablets		

1 Proceed exactly as for Vin Ordinaire. If a really astringent wine is preferred, tannin may be added before fermentation.

Comment
*Burgundy-type cultured yeast could be used if preferred.

Carnation & raisin wine

Classification: Table, Medium, Red

INGREDIENTS	UK/US	METRIC
Carnation flowers, red, scented	½ gallon	2.3 litres
Sultanas (or white raisins)	6oz	170g
Lemon, 1		
Orange, 1		
Sugar	3lb	1.36kg
Citric acid	¼oz	7g
Tannin, 2 to 3 drops or	1/16oz	1.75g
Yeast, all-purpose		

Yeast nutrient
Campden tablets

1 Follow the method for Rose Petal Wine, exactly.

Carrot & citrus wine

Classification: Table, Medium, Rosé

INGREDIENTS	UK/US	METRIC
Carrots, large (but not old)	6lb	2.7kg
Oranges, 4		
Lemons, 4		
Raisins	8oz	227g
Sugar, Demerara or light brown	4lb	1.8kg
Tannin, 2 to 3 drops or	$\frac{1}{16}$oz	1.75g
Yeast, all-purpose		
Yeast nutrient		
Campden tablets		
Black pepper, ground	$\frac{1}{4}$oz	7g

1 Thoroughly wash the carrots, but do not peel them, and trim off the ends.
2 Grate the carrots and place them in a pan with 1¼ gallons (5.7 litres) of water.
3 Boil the mixture for 40 minutes.
4 When cool, strain the liquid into a pail, squeezing out as much juice from the carrots as possible.
5 Add the sugar and stir until dissolved.
6 Pare the zest from the citrus fruit and squeeze out the juice.
7 Chop up the raisins and deseed if necessary.
8 Add the citrus zest and juice, the raisins, pepper, tannin, yeast and nutrient; stir well.
9 Cover the pail and stand in a warm place; stir daily.
10 After two weeks, strain the must into a

fermentation vessel and seal with an airlock.
11 When fermentation is complete, rack the wine into a clean container, add one crushed Campden tablet and close the container with a bung or a safety lock.
12 Rack every two months, for six months, then less frequently till clear.

Celery wine

Classification: Table, Medium, White

INGREDIENTS	UK/US	METRIC
Celery,	4lb	1.8kg
Sultanas (or white raisins)	8oz	227g
Lemons, 2		
Sugar, light brown	3lb	1.36kg
Tannin, 2 to 3 drops or	$\frac{1}{16}$oz	1.75g
Yeast, all-purpose		
Yeast nutrient		
Citric acid	$\frac{1}{4}$oz	7g
Campden tablets		

1 Wash the celery thoroughly, discarding the leaves, but retaining both the white and green stems.
2 Cut the stems into short lengths, add water to cover and boil until tender.
3 Strain the liquor into a pail, and add the chopped sultanas and citric acid.
4 Make up to 1 gallon (4.5 litres) with hot water; squeeze the juice from the lemons.
5 Add the sugar and lemon juice, and stir until the sugar is fully dissolved.
6 When the must has cooled, add the yeast, nutrient and tannin.
7 Cover the pail and stand it in a warm place, stirring daily.
8 After 12 days, strain the must into a fermentation vessel and seal it with an airlock.
9 When fermentation is complete, rack into a clean container, add one crushed Campden tablet and close with a bung or safety lock.
10 Rack every two months till clear.

Cherry wine

Classification: Dessert, Sweet, Rosé

INGREDIENTS	UK/US	METRIC
Morello cherries, ripe	8lb	3.6kg
Sugar	3½lb	1.5kg
Citric acid	½oz	14g
Tannin, 2 to 3 drops or	$\frac{1}{16}$oz	1.75g
Yeast, all-purpose		
Yeast nutrient		
Campden tablets		
Pectin destroying enzyme		

1 Wash the fruit thoroughly and allow it to drain.

2 Place the fruit in a large pail and cover it with 1 gallon (4.5 litres) of cold water.

3 Add one crushed Campden tablet, the citric acid and tannin. Cover the pail with a cloth and allow it to stand for five days, gradually crushing the cherries.

4 Dissolve the sugar in a little hot water and add this to the pail, stirring well, then add the pectin destroying enzyme.

5 After a further five days, add the yeast and nutrient, cover the pail and stand it in a warm place, stirring daily.

6 After four more days, strain the must into a fermentation vessel and seal it with an airlock.

7 When fermentation is complete, rack the wine into a clean container, add one crushed Campden tablet and close it with a bung or safety lock.

8 Rack every two month till clear.

NELSON HARGREAVES

Clover & citrus wine

Classification: Table, Medium, White

INGREDIENTS	UK/US	METRIC
Pink clover flowers	$\frac{1}{2}$ gallon	2.3 litres
Lemons 2		
Oranges, 2		
Ginger root, 1 piece		
Sugar	3lb	1.36kg
Citric acid	$\frac{1}{2}$oz	14g
Tannin,		
2 to 3 drops or	$\frac{1}{16}$oz	1.75g
Yeast, all-purpose		
Yeast nutrient		
Campden tablets		
Pectin destroying enzyme		

1 Wash the flowers.
2 Pare the zest and squeeze the juice from the oranges and lemons. 'Bruise' the ginger.
3 Put the flowers, sugar, orange and lemon juice and zest, bruised ginger, citric acid and tannin, with 1 gallon (4.5 litres) of water, into a pan.
4 Bring the fluid to the boil and simmer for 30 minutes, stirring frequently, then strain it into a pail.
5 When the liquid is lukewarm, add the pectin destroying enzyme and cover the pail.
6 After 24 hours, add the yeast and nutrient, then stand the pail in a warm place for 14 days, stirring daily.
7 At the end of this period, strain into a fermentation vessel, and insert an airlock.
8 When fermentation is complete, rack the wine into a clean container, add one crushed Campden tablet and close it with a bung or safety lock.
9 Rack every two months till clear.

Sweet Cherry Wine is an excellent alternative for Madeira or Port at the end of a meal.

Cornmeal wine

Classification: Table, Medium, White

INGREDIENTS	UK/US	METRIC
Cornmeal	1lb	454g
Lemons, 2		
Oranges, 2		
Grape juice sweet concentrate (white), $\frac{1}{2}$ can	1lb 1$\frac{1}{2}$oz	492g
Sugar	1$\frac{1}{2}$lb	680g
Citric acid	$\frac{1}{2}$oz	14g
Yeast, all-purpose		
Yeast nutrient		
Campden tablets		

1 Squeeze the juice from the citus fruit.
2 Add this juice, the grape juice concentrate, the citric acid, sugar and cornmeal to a pail. Add $\frac{3}{4}$ gallon (3.4 litres) of very hot water and stir thoroughly until the sugar has dissolved.
3 Pour the complete contents of the pail into a fermentation vessel, add warm water to make up to 1 gallon (4.5 litres) then the yeast and nutrient; fit an airlock.
4 Stand the vessel in a warm place until fermentation ceases.
5 Rack into a clean container, add one crushed Campden tablet and close the container with a bung or safety lock.
6 Rack after four weeks, and before bottling.

Cyser

Classification: Table, Medium, White

INGREDIENTS	UK/US	METRIC
Dessert apples	1$\frac{1}{4}$lb	608g
Crab apples	1$\frac{1}{2}$lb	680g
Honey	3lb	1.36kg

Citric acid	$\frac{1}{4}$oz	7g
Tannin,		
2 to 3 drops or	$\frac{1}{16}$oz	1.75g
Yeast, all-purpose		
Yeast nutrient		
Campden tablets		

1 Wash the apples, cut out any bruised parts and remove the pips.
2 Mince the apples, then squeeze and strain the juice into a pail.
3 Add two crushed Campden tablets and stir these in.
4 Dissolve the honey in hot water and simmer for 5 minutes then add it to the pail, with the citric acid and tannin. Allow it to stand for 24 hours.
5 Make up to 1 gallon (4.5 litres) with hot water, then add the yeast and nutrient.
6 Cover the pail and stand it in a warm place, stirring daily.
7 After seven days, strain the juice into a fermentation vessel and fit an airlock.
8 When fermentation is complete, rack the wine into a clean container, add one crushed Campden tablet and close the container with a bung or safety lock.
9 Rack every two months, for six months, then less frequently as sediment forms.

Damson plum wine

Classification: Table, Dry, Red

INGREDIENTS	UK/US	METRIC
Damson plums	3lb	1.36kg
Sugar	2$\frac{1}{2}$lb	1.13kg
Citric acid	$\frac{1}{4}$oz	7g
Yeast, all-purpose		
Yeast nutrient		
Campden tablets		
Pectin destroying enzyme		

1 Wash the fruit gently, and drain it.
2 Put the fruit in a pail and pour over it $\frac{1}{4}$ gallon (1.14 litres) of boiling water.
3 Add 1lb (454g) of the sugar and citric acid. Stir until the sugar has dissolved and break up the fruit with a large spoon.
4 Add a further $\frac{1}{2}$ gallon (2.3 litres) of warm water, then add the pectin destroying enzyme; cover the pail and stand it in a warm place, stirring daily.
5 After two days, strain it into a fermentation vessel, then dissolve 1$\frac{1}{2}$lb (454g) of sugar in hot water and add this to the vessel.
6 Add the yeast and nutrient, then make up to 1 gallon (4.5 litres) with warm water and seal the vessel with an airlock.
7 When fermentation is complete, rack into a clean container, add one crushed Campden tablet and close the container with a bung or safety lock.
8 Rack every two months till clear.

Dandelion wine

Classification: Table, Medium, White

INGREDIENTS	UK/US	METRIC
Dandelion flowers	$\frac{3}{4}$ gallon	3.4 litres
Lemon, 1		
Orange, 1		
Ginger root, 1 piece		
Sugar	3lb	1.36kg
Citric acid	$\frac{1}{4}$oz	7g
Tannin,		
2 to 3 drops or	$\frac{1}{16}$oz	1.75g

Yeast, all-purpose
Yeast nutrient
Campden tablets
Pectin destroying
enzyme

1 Wash the flowers thoroughly and drain them.
2 Put the flowers in a pail and cover them with 1 gallon (4.5 litres) of boiling water.
3 Cover the pail and leave it for three days, stirring daily.
4 Pare the zest from the citrus fruit and squeeze out the juice; 'bruise' the ginger root.
5 Thoroughly squeeze out the flowers into a pan, then add the citrus zest and juice, ginger root, citric acid, tannin and sugar. Stir well to dissolve the sugar while bringing to the boil.
6 Boil for 30 minutes, then pour into a pail.
7 When cool, add the pectin destroying enzyme; cover the container and stand it in a warm place.
8 After 24 hours, add the yeast and yeast nutrient. Stir daily.
9 After six days, strain the liquor into a fermentation vessel and seal it.
10 When fermentation is complete, rack the wine into a clean container, add one crushed Campden tablet and close it with a bung or safety lock.
11 Rack every two months, for six months, then rack again as the sediment settles.

Elderberry punch

Classification: For winter nights

INGREDIENTS	UK/US	METRIC
Elderberry wine, 2 bottles		
Brandy	4fl oz	114ml
Oranges, 4		

Lemons, 2		
Cloves	¼oz	7g
Sugar (to taste)		
Cinnamon stick	½ oz	14g

1 Pare the zest from the oranges and lemons, and squeeze out the juice. Put the cloves and cinnamon in a muslin or cheesecloth bag.
2 Put the zest and the juice into a jug, together with the bag of spices and the wine.
3 Stand the jug in a warm place for two hours, then strain the punch into a pan.
4 Heat, but do not overheat, or the alcohol will evaporate.
5 Add the brandy and serve hot, with sugar added to taste.

Elderberry wine

Classification: Dessert, Sweet, Red

INGREDIENTS	UK/US	METRIC
Ripe elderberries	4lb	1.8kg
Raisins	8oz	227g
Ginger root, 1 piece		
Lemon, 1		
Sugar	3lb	1.36kg
Citric acid	¼oz	7g
Yeast, all-purpose		
Yeast nutrient		
Campden tablets		

Pectin destroying enzyme

1 Wash the sprays of berries thoroughly, then strip the berries from their stalks.
2 Boil the berries in 1 gallon (4.5 litres) of water, for 10 minutes.
3 Squeeze the juice from the lemon, chop and deseed the raisins and 'bruise' the ginger.
4 Strain the juice from the berries and return the juice to the pan.
5 Add the raisins, sugar, lemon juice, citric acid and bruised ginger, then simmer together for 20 minutes.
6 When the mixture is cool, transfer it to a pail and add the pectin destroying enzyme; cover the pail.
7 After 24 hours, add the yeast and nutrient.
8 Stand the pail in a warm place for three weeks, stirring daily.
9 At the end of this period, strain the juice into a fermentation vessel and fit an airlock.
10 When fermentation is complete, rack into a clean container with one crushed Campden tablet, and close the container with a bung or safety lock.
11 Rack every two months till clear before bottling.

Gluwein is a good warming drink in cold weather.

Gluwein

Classification: For the winter nights

INGREDIENTS	UK/US	METRIC
Red wine, 1 bottle		
Mulling spices, 1 packet		
Sugar	2oz	57g

1 Tie the spices in a muslin or cheesecloth bag, then put them in a pan with the wine and sugar.
2 Heat the wine, but do not overheat, or the alcohol will evaporate. Taste occasionally removing the spices when their flavour is sufficiently strong.

Gooseberry (green) wine

Classification: Table, Dry, White

INGREDIENTS	UK/US	METRIC
Gooseberries, green and ripe	4lb	1.8kg
Sugar	2½lb	1.13kg
Citric acid	¼oz	7g
Tannin, 2 to 3 drops or	$\frac{1}{16}$oz	1.75g
Yeast, all-purpose		
Yeast nutrient		
Campden tablets		
Pectin destroying enzyme		

1 'Top and tail' and wash the gooseberries.
2 Put the gooseberries in a pail and add ½ gallon (2.3 litres) of hot water.
3 Cover and stand the pail for three days, mashing daily.
4 Dissolve the sugar in some hot water.
5 Strain the liquid from the gooseberries and add, with the sugar syrup, the tannin, citric acid and pectin destroying enzyme, to the fermentation vessel, stir thoroughly.
6 After 24 hours add the yeast and nutrient, make up to 1 gallon (4.5 litres) of water and seal the vessel with an airlock.
7 When fermentation is complete, rack the wine into a clean container, add one crushed Campden tablet and close the container with a bung or safety lock.
8 Rack every two months till clear.

Grapefruit juice wine

Classification: Dessert, Sweet, White

INGREDIENTS	UK/US	METRIC
Grapefruit juice, 1 can (sweetened)*	1lb 3oz	538g
Orange, 1		
Lemon, 1		
Sugar	2½lb	1.13kg
Tannin, 2 to 3 drops or	$\frac{1}{16}$oz	1.75g
Yeast, all-purpose		
Yeast nutrient		
Campden tablets		
Pectin destroying enzyme		

1 Pare the zest from the orange and lemon, and squeeze out the juice.
2 Dissolve the sugar in hot water and pour it into the fermentation vessel.
3 Add the citrus zest and juice, and grapefruit juice.

4 Add the tannin and pectin destroying enzyme, with ½ gallon (2.3 litres) of warm water.
5 After 24 hours, add the yeast and yeast nutrient; make up to 1 gallon (4.5 litres).
6 Seal the vessel with an airlock, and stand it in a warm place.
7 When fermentation is complete, rack the wine into a clean container, add one crushed Campden tablet and seal it with a bung or safety lock.
8 Rack after three weeks, and again before bottling.

Comment
*If unsweetened juice is used, add 3lb (1.36kg) of sugar.

Greengage wine

Classification: Table, Medium, White

INGREDIENTS	UK/US	METRIC
Greengage plums, ripe	3lb	1.36kg
Ground barley	6oz	170g
Sugar	3lb	1.36kg

Citric acid	¼oz	7g
Tannin,		
2 to 3 drops or	$\frac{1}{16}$oz	1.75g
Yeast, cereal-type		
Yeast nutrient		
Campden tablets		
Pectin destroying enzyme		

1 Rinse the fruit gently, and allow it to drain.
2 Put the fruit in a pail with the barley and pour 1 gallon (4.5 litres) of boiling water into the pail. Cover it and leave for four days.
3 At the end of this period, strain the liquid into a second pail, and add the sugar, citric acid, tannin and pectin destroying enzyme. Stir well to dissolve the sugar, and cover the pail.
4 After 24 hours, add the yeast and nutrient, stir again, and stand the pail in a warm place. Stir daily.
5 After seven days, strain the must into a fermentation vessel and seal it with an airlock.
6 When fermentation is complete, rack the wine into a container, add one crushed Campden tablet and close it with a bung or safety lock.
7 Rack every two months till clear.

Hock wine

Classification: Table, Dry, White

INGREDIENTS	UK/US	METRIC
Hock grape juice concentrate, 1 can	2lb 3oz	1kg
Sugar	10oz	284g
Yeast, all-purpose*		
Yeast nutrient		
Campden tablets		

1 Proceed exactly as for Vin Ordinaire.

Comment
*Hock-Type cultured yeast could be used if preferred.

Honeysuckle wine

Classification: Table, Medium, White

INGREDIENTS	UK/US	METRIC
Honeysuckle blossom	2 pints	1.14 litres
Raisins	4oz	113g
Lemon, 1		
Orange, 1		
Sugar	3lb	1.36kg
Citric acid	¼oz	7g
Tannin,		
2 to 3 drops or	$\frac{1}{16}$oz	1.75g
Yeast, all-purpose		
Yeast nutrient		
Campden tablets		

1 Wash the flowers gently and drain them.
2 Deseed and chop the raisins, pare the zest from the citrus fruit and squeeze the juice from it.
3 Place the flowers, raisins, zest and juice from the fruit in a pail and add a crushed Campden tablet.
4 Add 1 gallon (4.5 litres) of hot water to the pail, stir well, cover it and leave for 24 hours.
5 Dissolve the sugar in hot water and add this to the must with the citric acid and tannin.

6 Add the yeast and nutrient, stir well, cover the pail and stand it in a warm place.

7 After seven days, strain the must into a fermentation vessel and seal it.

8 When fermentation has ceased, rack the wine into a clean container, add one crushed Campden tablet and close it with a bung or safety lock.

9 Rack every two months till clear.

Loganberry wine

Classification: Table, Medium, Rosé

INGREDIENTS	UK/US	METRIC
Loganberries	4lb	1.8kg
Sugar, light brown	3lb	1.36kg
Citric acid	$\frac{1}{4}$oz	7g
Yeast, all-purpose		
Yeast nutrient		
Campden tablets		
Pectin destroying enzyme		

1 Follow the same method as for Blackberry Wine, omitting the lemon and tannin.

Marigold wine

Classification: Table, Medium, White

INGREDIENTS	UK/US	METRIC
Marigold flowers (heads)	$\frac{3}{4}$ gallon	3.4 litres
Lemons, 2		
Sugar	3lb	1.36kg
Tannin, 2 to 3 drops or	$\frac{1}{16}$oz	1.75g
Yeast, all-purpose		
Yeast nutrient		
Campden tablets		

1 Thoroughly wash the flowers, and drain them.

2 Dissolve the sugar in a little hot water.

3 Pare the zest from the lemons and squeeze out the juice.

4 Put the flowers, sugar, tannin, lemon zest and juice into a pail and make up to 1 gallon (4.5 litres) with hot water.

5 When the mixture has cooled, add the yeast and nutrient.

6 Cover the pail and stand it in a warm place, stirring daily.

7 After seven days, strain the must into a fermentation vessel and close it with an airlock.

8 When fermentation is complete, rack into a clean container, add one crushed Campden tablet and close the container with a bung or safety lock.

9 Rack every two months till clear.

Mead

Classification: Table, Dry, White

INGREDIENTS	UK/US	METRIC
Honey (light)	3lb	1.36kg
Orange, 1		
Lemon, 1		
Sugar cubes– 1 per bottle		
Citric acid	$\frac{1}{2}$oz	14g
Tannin, 2 to 3 drops or	$\frac{1}{16}$oz	1.75g
Yeast, all-purpose		

Yeast nutrient
Campden tablets

1 Put the honey into a pan and add hot water to make up to 1 gallon (4.5 litres).
2 Stir well over heat until the honey has melted, then retain a low heat for a further five minutes.
3 Squeeze the lemon and orange, retaining the juice.
4 Add to the melted honey the lemon and orange juice, the tannin, citric acid, the yeast and the nutrient.
5 Strain the liquid into a fermentation vessel, stand it in a warm place and plug the vessel with cotton wool (absorbant cotton).
6 After four days, fit a fermentation lock.
7 When fermentation is complete, rack into a clean container, add one crushed Campden tablet and close the container with a bung or safety lock.
8 When cleared, rack into strong bottles (screw top beer bottles or champagne bottles), add a cube of sugar to each bottle and close them. Tie down the corks or stoppers.

Melomel

Classification: Dessert, Sweet, Red

INGREDIENTS	UK/US	METRIC
Blackcurrants	3lb	1.36kg
Honey, light	4lb	1.8kg
Lemons, 2		
Yeast, all-purpose		
Yeast nutrient		
Campden tablets		
Pectin destroying enzyme ·		

1 Strip the blackcurrants from their stalks, then wash and drain them.
2 Pare the zest from the lemons and squeeze out the juice.
3 Put the currants into a pail, crush them, add the pectin destroying enzyme, the zest

and juice of the lemons and one crushed Campden tablet.
4 Add 6 pints (3.4 litres) of cold water to the pail, stir well, cover it and leave it for 24 hours.
5 Dissolve the honey in a little hot water and simmer for five minutes. Add this to the pail.
6 Stir in the yeast and yeast nutrient, cover the pail and stand it in a warm place for two days, stirring daily.
7 Strain the must into a fermentation vessel, add water to make 1 gallon (4.5 litres) and seal the vessel with an airlock.
8 When fermentation is complete, rack the wine into a clean container, add one crushed Campden tablet and close the container with a bung or safety lock.
9 Rack every two months, for six months, then less frequently as sediment forms.

Comment
Any fruit, except apples, can be mixed with the honey to make melomel. A less strongly flavoured fruit such as rose hips, with 1lb (454g) less honey, will make a dry melomel.

Mixed dried fruit wine

Classification: Dessert, Sweet, White

INGREDIENTS	UK/US	METRIC
Raisins	4oz	113g
Currants	4oz	113g
Sultanas (or white raisins)	2 oz	57g
Candied peel	2oz	57g
Whole wheat grains	1lb	454g
Sugar	3lb	1.36kg
Citric acid	$\frac{1}{2}$oz	14g
Tannin, 2 to 3 drops or	$\frac{1}{16}$oz	1.75g
Yeast, cereal-type		
Yeast nutrient		
Campden tablets		

Pectin destroying enzyme

1 Wash and chop up the currants, sultanas and raisins, deseeding if necessary.
2 Put this dried fruit with the candied peel, sugar and wheat in a pail.
3 Pour 1 gallon (4.5 litres) boiling water into the pail and stir well until all the sugar has dissolved.
4 Add the citric acid, tannin and pectin destroying enzyme to the pail. Cover it and leave for 24 hours.
5 Add the yeast and nutrient, then stand the pail in a warm place for three weeks.
6 Strain the must into a fermentation jar and seal it with an airlock.
7 When fermentation has ceased, rack the wine into a clean container with one crushed Campden tablet, and close the container with a bung or safety lock.
8 Rack every two month till clear.

Nettle wine

Classification: Table, Medium, White

INGREDIENTS	UK/US	METRIC
Nettles (tops only, young)	½ gallon	2.3 litres
Lemons, 1		
Ginger root, 1 piece		
Sugar	3lb	1.8kg
Citric acid	½oz	14g
Tannin, 2 to 3 drops or	$\frac{1}{16}$oz	1.75g
Yeast		
Yeast nutrient		
Campden tablets		

1 Wash the nettle tops, and allow them to drain.
2 Pare the zest from the lemons and squeeze out the juice.
3 Bruise the ginger root.
4 Put the nettles, lemon zest and juice and

the ginger root into a pan with water to cover them. Bring to the boil and simmer for 30 minutes.
5 Dissolve the sugar in a little hot water.
6 Strain the liquid from the pan into a pail, add the sugar syrup, citric acid and tannin.
7 Add warm water to make up to 1 gallon (4.5 litres), add the yeast and nutrient, cover the pail and stand it in a warm place, stirring daily.
8 After seven days, rack the must into a fermentation vessel and seal it with an airlock.
9 When fermentation is complete, rack the wine into a container, add one crushed Campden tablet and close the container with a bung or safety lock.
10 Rack every two months till clear.

Oakleaf wine

Classification: Table, Medium, White

INGREDIENTS	UK/US	METRIC
Oakleaves, green	1 gallon	4.5 litres
Lemons, 2		
Sugar	3½lb	1.59kg
Citric acid	¼oz	7g
Yeast, all-purpose		
Yeast nutrient		
Campden tablets		

1 Wash the leaves thoroughly and drain them.
2 Boil ¾ gallon (3.4 litres) of water and add

the sugar; stir until dissolved.

3 Put the leaves into a pail and pour the boiling liquid over them. Cover and leave to stand for 24 hours.

4 Squeeze the juice from the lemons; add this juice and the citric acid to the pail and stir well.

5 Strain into a fermentation vessel and add the yeast and nutrient, and warm water to make up to 1 gallon (4.5 litres).

6 Seal the vessel with an airlock and stand it in a warm place.

7 When fermentation is complete, rack the wine into a clean container, add one crushed Campden tablet, and seal the container with a bung or safety lock.

8 Rack every two months till clear.

Orange & sultana wine

Classification: Dessert, Sweet*, White

INGREDIENTS	UK/US	METRIC
Oranges, sweet, to make 2 pints juice		
Lemons, 2		
Sultanas (or white raisins)	1lb	454g
Sugar	4lb	1.8kg
Tannin, 2 to 3 drops or	$\frac{1}{16}$oz	1.75g
Yeast, all-purpose		
Yeast nutrient		
Campden tablets		
Pectin destroying enzyme		

1 Pare the zest from the oranges and lemons and squeeze out the juice.

2 Deseed and chop the sultanas, then put them into a pail with the orange and lemon juice.

3 Put the zest of the oranges and lemons into a small bowl, add $\frac{1}{2}$ pint (284ml) of boiling

50

water and crush the zest with the back of a spoon. Allow to stand for an hour, then strain the liquid into the pail.

4 Dissolve the sugar and add the tannin and pectin destroying enzyme. Make up to 1 gallon (4.5 litres) then cover the pail and stand it in a warm place.

5 After 24 hours, add the yeast and nutrient.

6 After three more days, strain into a fermentation vessel and fit an airlock.

7 When fermentation is complete, rack into a clean container, add one crushed Campden tablet and close the container with a bung or safety lock.

8 Rack after two months, and again later if necessary.

Comment

If the wine is made without the orange and lemon zest, a rather tasteless result is produced. This would serve excellently as the wine basis for an orange liqueur, however. *For a dry wine use 2½lb (1.13kg) sugar.

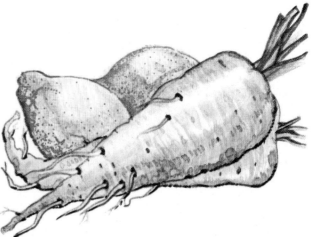

Parsnip wine

Classification: Table, Medium, White

INGREDIENTS	UK/US	METRIC
Parsnips	5lb	2.27kg
Lemon, 1		

Sugar	3lb	1.36kg
Citric acid	$\frac{1}{2}$oz	14g
Tannin,		
2 to 3 drops or	$\frac{1}{16}$oz	1.75g
Yeast, all-purpose		
Yeast nutrient		
Campden tablets		
Pectin destroying enzyme		

1 Wash and peel the parsnips, cut them into small pieces and boil them until tender in 1 gallon (4.5 litres) of water.
2 Strain off the water into a pail, but do not squeeze or press the parsnips, or the wine will be cloudy.
3 Pare the lemon to remove the zest, and squeeze out the juice.
4 Add the lemon zest and juice, the citric acid, pectin destroying enzyme, tannin and a crushed Campden tablet to the pail.
5 Dissolve the sugar in a little hot water and add the syrup to the pail. Allow it to stand for 24 hours.
6 Add the yeast and nutrient, stir well, cover the pail and stand it in a warm place,
7 Stir daily; after 2 weeks, strain the must into a fermentation jar and seal it with an airlock.
8 When fermentation is complete, rack the wine into a clean container, add one crushed Campden tablet and close the container with a bung or safety lock.
9 Rack after two months and again before bottling.

Peach (canned) wine

Classification: Table, Medium, White

INGREDIENTS	UK/US	METRIC
Canned peach halves, slices or pulp	2lb	907g

Sugar	$2\frac{1}{2}$lb	1.13kg
Citric acid	$\frac{1}{2}$oz	14g
Tannin,		
2 to 3 drops or	$\frac{1}{16}$oz	1.75g
Yeast, all-purpose		
Yeast nutrient		
Campden tablets		
Pectin destroying enzyme		

1 If the peaches are in halves or pieces, cut them up.
2 Boil a kettleful of water and dissolve the sugar to form a syrup.
3 Mix together the sugar syrup, the syrup from the peach can, and the peaches, in a pail, then add $\frac{3}{4}$ gallon (3.4 litres) of hot water. Stir well.
4 Add the citric acid, tannin and pectin destroying enzyme. Stir again, cover and stand the mixture in a warm place for 24 hours.
5 Add the yeast and nutrient, stir, cover and stand it in a warm place, stirring daily for 10 days.
6 Strain the must into a fermentation jar and seal this with an airlock.
7 When fermentation is complete, rack the wine into a clean container, add one crushed Campden tablet and close the container with a bung or safety lock.
8 Rack after two months, and again before bottling.

Pea pod wine

Classification: Table, Medium, White

INGREDIENTS	UK/US	METRIC
Pea pods, young	$4\frac{1}{2}$lb	2kg
Sugar	3lb	1.36kg
Citric acid	$\frac{1}{4}$oz	7g
Tannin,		
2 to 3 drops or	$\frac{1}{16}$oz	1.75g
Yeast		

Yeast nutrient
Campden tablets
Pectin destroying
enzyme

1 Wash and drain the pea pods.
2 Put the pea pods into a pan, add a crushed Campden tablet and 1 gallon (4.5 litres) of water and boil until the pods are tender.
3 Strain the water into a pail and add the sugar, citric acid, tannin and pectin destroying enzyme.
4 Stir thoroughly until the sugar has dissolved. Allow to stand for 24 hours.
5 Add the yeast and nutrient, stir again, cover the pail and stand it in a warm place.
6 Stir daily; after three days, strain the must into a fermentation jar and seal it with an airlock.
7 When fermentation is complete, rack the wine into a clean container, add one crushed Campden tablet and close it with a bung or safety lock.
8 Rack every two months till clear.

Pineapple (canned) wine

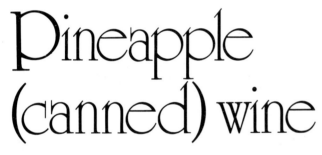

Classification: Table, Medium to dry, White

1 Proceed exactly as for Peach (canned) Wine, but substituting 2lb (907g) canned pineapple slices or chunks.

Plum wine

Classification: Table, Medium, Rosé

INGREDIENTS	UK/US	METRIC
Plums, red or black, ripe	6lb	2.7kg
Sugar	3lb	1.36kg

Citric acid	$\frac{1}{4}$oz	7g
Tannin, 2 to 3 drops or	$\frac{1}{16}$oz	1.75g
Yeast, all-purpose		
Yeast nutrient		
Campden tablets		
Pectin destroying enzyme		

1 Wash the fruit thoroughly and drain it.
2 Place the fruit in 1 gallon (4.5 litres) of boiling water and simmer it for 10 minutes, then transfer to a pail.
3 Add the sugar, citric acid, tannin, a crushed Campden tablet and the pectin destroying enzyme. Stir until the sugar has dissolved. Leave for 24 hours, covered.
4 Add the yeast and nutrient, stir well, cover the pail and stand it in a warm place, stirring daily.
5 After three days, strain into a fermentation vessel and fit an airlock.
6 When fermentation is complete, rack the wine into a container, add one crushed Campden tablet and close it with a bung or safety lock.
7 Rack every two months till clear.

Pomegranate & barley wine

Classification: Table, Medium, White

INGREDIENTS	UK/US	METRIC
Pomegranates, 10		
Barley	8oz	227g
Lemon, 1		
Sugar	3lb	1.36kg
Citric acid	$\frac{1}{2}$oz	14g
Tannin, 2 to 3 drops or	$\frac{1}{16}$oz	1.75g
Yeast, cereal-type		
Yeast nutrient		
Campden tablets		
Pectin destroying enzyme		

1 Put the barley in a pan with ½ gallon (2.3 litres) of water, bring it slowly to the boil and simmer for 5 minutes.
2 Split open the pomegranates and scrape the seeds into a pail.
3 Squeeze the juice from the lemon and add this juice, the citric acid, tannin, pectin destroying enzyme and sugar to the pail.
4 Strain the water from the barley into the pail and stir until the sugar has dissolved.
5 Make up the mixture with warm water to 1 gallon (4.5 litres) and stand for 24 hours. Add the yeast and nutrient.
6 Cover the pail and stand it in a warm place for five days, stirring daily.
7 At the end of this period strain into a fermentation vessel and seal with an airlock.
8 When fermentation is complete, rack the wine into a clean container, add one crushed Campden tablet and close it with a bung or safety lock.
9 Rack every two months till clear.

Pyment

Classification: Table, Medium, White

INGREDIENTS	UK/US	METRIC
Grape juice concentrate, ½ can	1lb 2oz	510g
Honey (pale)	2½lb	1.13kg
Yeast, all-purpose		
Yeast nutrient		
Campden tablets		

1 Dissolve the honey in hot water and simmer for 5 minutes, then pour directly into the fermentation vessel.
2 Add the grape concentrate then add warm water to make up to 1 gallon (4.5 litres). Stir well.
3 Add the yeast and nutrient, seal the fermentation vessel with an airlock and stand it in a warm place.
4 When fermentation is complete, rack the wine into a clean container, add one crushed Campden tablet and close the container with a bung or safety lock.
5 Rack every two months for six months, then less frequently as sediment forms.

Comment
If fresh grapes are available, press the juice from 3lb (1.36kg), and increase the honey to 3½ lb (1.59kg).

Raspberry wine

Classification: Table, Medium, Rosé

INGREDIENTS	UK/US	METRIC
Raspberries, ripe	4lb	1.8kg
Sugar	3½lb	1.59kg
Citric acid	¼oz	7g
Yeast, all-purpose		
Yeast nutrient		
Campden tablets		
Pectin destroying enzyme		

1 Wash the raspberries gently and drain them.
2 Put the fruit into a pail, add ¾ gallon (3.4 litres) of boiling water and crush the fruit completely.

3 Cover the pail and leave it for four days, stirring daily.

4 Dissolve the sugar in a little hot water, then add this syrup, the citric acid and pectin destroying enzyme.

5 Add warm water to make up to 1 gallon (4.5 litres). After 24 hours add the yeast and nutrient; cover the pail and stand it in a warm place.

6 After two days, strain the liquid into a fermentation vessel and seal this with an airlock.

7 When fermentation is complete, rack the wine into a clean container, add one crushed Campden tablet and close the container with a bung or safety lock.

8 Rack after two months, and before bottling.

Rhubarb wine

Classification: Table, Medium, Rosé

INGREDIENTS	UK/US	METRIC
Rhubarb (red and ripe, but not the pink forced early rhubarb)	6lb	2.7kg
Lemons, 2		
Sugar	3½lb	1.59kg
Tannin, 2 to 3 drops or	$\frac{1}{16}$oz	1.75g
Yeast, all-purpose		
Yeast nutrient		
Campden tablets		
Pectin destroying enzyme		
Precipitated chalk	½oz	14g

1 Discard all the rhubarb leaves, which are poisonous.

2 Wash the rhubarb and drain it, cut it up into small pieces, crush it in a pail and cover it with ¾ gallon (3.4 litres) of cold water.

3 Add a crushed Campden tablet, stir this in, and leave for three days.

4 Strain the juice into a second pail and add the precipitated chalk. The wine will fizz as excess oxalic acid is neutralized.

5 Pare the zest from the lemons and squeeze out the juice.

6 Add the lemon zest and juice, the tannin and the pectin destroying enzyme to the pail.

7 Dissolve the sugar in a little hot water and add the syrup to the other ingredients. Make up to 1 gallon (4.5 litres) with water.

8 After 24 hours add the yeast and nutrient, cover the pail and stand it in a warm place. Stir daily.

9 After three days, strain it into a fermentation vessel and seal this with an airlock.

10 When fermentation is complete, rack the wine into a container, add one crushed Campden tablet and seal the container with a bung or safety lock.

11 Rack every two months till clear.

Rhubarb & beetroot (beet) wine

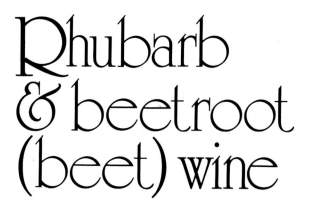

Classification: Table, Medium, Red

INGREDIENTS	UK/US	METRIC
Rhubarb	3lb	1.36kg
Beetroot (beet)	3lb	1.36kg
Whole wheat grains	1lb	454g
Raisins	8oz	227g
Sugar	3lb	1.8kg
Tannin, 2 to 3 drops or	$\frac{1}{16}$oz	1.75g
Yeast, cereal-type		
Yeast nutrient		
Ginger root, 1 piece		

Campden tablets		
Pectin destroying		
enzyme		
Precipitated chalk	$\frac{1}{2}$oz	14g

1 Cut the rhubarb into small pieces, discarding all leaves, which are poisonous.
2 Put the rhubarb into a pail and pour $\frac{1}{2}$ gallon (2.3 litres) of boiling water over it.
3 Sprinkle the precipitated chalk over the rhubarb; it will fizz, releasing excess oxalic acid.
4 Add one crushed Campden tablet and allow it to stand for 10 days, stirring and pressing the rhubarb every day, then strain it into a second pail.
5 Slice the beetroot, unpeeled, into $\frac{1}{2}$ gallon (2.3 litres) of hot water. When soft (in about 2 days), strain into the pail with the rhubarb juice.
6 Deseed and chop the raisins, 'bruise' the root ginger and add with the wheat, pectin destroying enzyme, tannin, sugar and raisins to the pail. Stir well to dissolve the sugar.
7 After 24 hours add the yeast and nutrient, then cover the pail and allow the must to ferment for four to five days, stirring daily.
8 Strain the liquid into a fermentation vessel and fit an airlock.
9 When fermentation is complete, rack into a clean container, add one crushed Campden tablet, and close the container with a bung or safety lock.
10 Rack every two months till clear.

Rice & raisin wine

Classification: Table, Medium, White

INGREDIENTS	UK/US	METRIC
Rice (unpolished or paddy)	1lb	454g
Raisins	1lb	454g
Lemon, 1		

Sugar	3lb	1.36kg
Tannin, 2 to 3 drops or	$\frac{1}{16}$oz	1.75g
Yeast, cereal-type		
Yeast nutrient		
Campden tablets		

1 Chop and deseed the raisins.
2 Pare the zest from the lemon, and squeeze out the juice.
3 Put the rice, chopped deseeded raisins, tannin, zest and juice of the lemon into a pail and add 1 gallon (4.5 litres) of boiling water.
4 Add the sugar and stir well until dissolved.
5 Add the yeast and nutrient, stir again, cover the pail and stand it in a warm place. Stir daily.
6 After seven days, strain the must into a fermentation vessel and seal it with an airlock.
7 When fermentation is complete, rack the wine into a clean container, add one crushed Campden tablet and close it with a bung or safety lock.
8 Rack every two months till clear.

Rose hip wine

Classification: Table, Medium, Rosé

INGREDIENTS	UK/US	METRIC
Rose hips, fully ripe	6 pints	3.4 litres
Orange, 1		
Sugar	3lb	1.36kg
Citric acid	$\frac{1}{2}$oz	14g
Tannin, 2 to 3 drops or	$\frac{1}{16}$oz	1.75g
Yeast, all-purpose		
Yeast nutrient		
Campden tablets		
Pectin destroying enzyme		

1 Wash the rose hips, drain, then crush them with a wooden mallet.
2 Place the hips in a pail and add ¾ gallon (3.4 litres) of boiling water.
3 Pare the zest from the orange and squeeze out the juice.
4 Add one crushed Campden tablet, and the zest and juice of the orange, to the pail. Allow it to stand for 24 hours.
5 Dissolve the sugar in a little hot water and add the syrup to the pail.
6 Add the citric acid, tannin, and pectin destroying enzyme. Stir well and cover the pail.
7 After 24 hours, add the yeast and nutrient. Stand the pail in a warm place for three days.
8 Make up the must to one gallon with warm water, strain into a fermentation vessel and seal this with an airlock.
9 When fermentation is complete, rack the wine into a clean container, add one crushed Campden tablet, and close the container with a bung or safety lock.
10 Rack every two months, for six months, then less frequently as sediment forms.

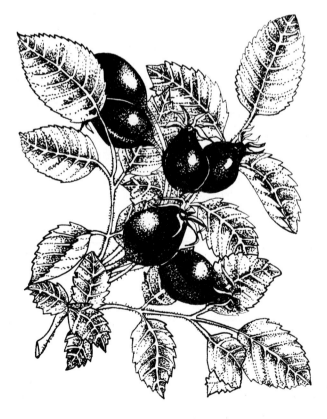

Rose petal wine

Classification: Table, Medium, White

INGREDIENTS	UK/US	METRIC
Rose petals (red, scented are best)	4 pints	2.3 litres
Sultanas (or white raisins)	6oz	170g
Lemon, 1		
Orange, 1		
Sugar	3lb	1.36kg
Citric acid	¼oz	7g
Tannin, 2 to 3 drops or	$\frac{1}{16}$oz	1.75g
Yeast, all-purpose		
Yeast nutrient		
Campden tablets		

1 Wash the petals thoroughly.
2 Pare the zest from the orange and lemon, and squeeze out the juice.
3 Chop and deseed the sultanas.
4 Add together in a pail the rose petals, sugar, orange and lemon zest and juice, and the sultanas. Cover these with 1 gallon (4.5 litres) of boiling water.
5 Stir well to dissolve the sugar.
6 When lukewarm, add the citric acid, tannin yeast and nutrient.
7 Cover the pail and stand it in a warm place, stirring daily.
8 After seven days, strain the must into a fermentation vessel, and seal this with an airlock.
9 When fermentation is complete, rack the wine into a storage container, add one crushed Campden tablet and close the container with a bung or safety lock.
10 Rack every two months, for six months, then less frequently as sediment forms.

Sangria is a popular summer drink.

Sangria

Classification: Summer cup

INGREDIENTS	UK/US	METRIC
Red or white wine, 2 bottles		
Orange, 1		
Lemon, 1		
Sugar	8oz	227g

1 Slice the orange and lemon thinly, and place half of each in two glass jugs, about 3 hours before the Sangria will be required.
2 Add the wine to the fruit — one jug of white and one of red looks attractive on the table.
3 Taste before serving — if required, add a little sugar and stir well.
4 Finally, add a few ice cubes.

'Sherry' wine

Classification: Aperitif, Medium, Red

INGREDIENTS	UK/US	METRIC
Sherry grape juice concentrate, 1 can	2lb 3oz	1kg
Sugar	12oz	340g
Yeast, all-purpose*		
Yeast nutrient		
Campden tablets		
Vodka, 100° proof	3fl oz	85ml

1 Proceed exactly as the Vin Ordinaire recipe.
2 When the wine is matured it will have a sherry flavour, but real sherry is fortified.
3 If you like what you have made, put 3fl oz (85ml) of 100° proof Vodka into a wine bottle and fill it with the 'sherry'. Seal the bottle and leave it for a few days before use.

Comment
*Sherry-type cultured yeast could be tried for this recipe.

Sloe wine

Classification: Dessert, Sweet, Red

INGREDIENTS	UK/US	METRIC
Sloes	3½lb	1.59kg
Raisins	8oz	227g
Sugar	3½lb	1.59kg
Yeast, all-purpose		
Yeast nutrient		
Campden tablets		
Pectin destroying enzyme		

1 Wash the sloes gently and drain them.
2 Put the sloes into a pail and cover them with ¾ gallon (3.4 litres) of boiling water. Cover the pail with a cloth.

3 Let the sloes soak for a day, then mash them well.

4 Chop and deseed the raisins, and add them and the pectin destroying enzyme to the pail.

5 Dissolve the sugar in a little boiling water, and add this to the pail. Add a further $\frac{1}{4}$ gallon (1.14 litres) of hot water and stir well. Stand for 24 hours.

6 Add the yeast and nutrient, cover the pail and stand it in a warm place.

7 After 10 days, strain the must into a fermentation vessel and seal this with an airlock.

8 When fermentation is complete, rack the wine into a container, add one crushed Campden tablet and close the container with a bung or safety lock.

9 Rack every two months, for six months, then less frequently as sediment forms.

Strawberry wine

Classification: Table, Medium*, Rosé

INGREDIENTS	UK/US	METRIC
Strawberries, ripe	4lb	1.8kg
Sugar	3lb	1.36kg
Citric acid	$\frac{1}{2}$oz	$\frac{1}{4}$g
Tannin,		
2 to 3 drops or	$\frac{1}{16}$oz	1.75g
Yeast, all-purpose		
Yeast nutrient		
Campden tablets		
Pectin destroying enzyme		

1 Hull the strawberries, wash them well and allow them to drain.

2 Dissolve the sugar in a little hot water, add the strawberries and mash them thoroughly.

3 Add $\frac{1}{2}$ gallon (2.3 litres) of warm water and leave in a covered pail for two days.

4 Add the citric acid, tannin and pectin destroying enzyme. Stand for 24 hours.

5 Add a further $\frac{1}{2}$ gallon (2.3 litres) of warm water, stir well and strain into the fermentation vessel.

6 Add the yeast and yeast nutrient, and seal the vessel with an airlock.

7 When fermentation is complete, strain the must into a container, add one crushed Campden tablet and close the container with a bung or safety lock.

8 Rack after two months and again before bottling.

Comment
*Makes an excellent dry wine using 2½lb (1.13kg) of sugar.

Strawberries make a delicious dry wine.

MICHAEL BOYS/SUSAN GRIGGS AGENCY